142706

D'Agostino.
Olives on the apple tree.

The Italian American Experience

OLIVES
ON
THE APPLE
TREE

GUIDO D'AGOSTINO

ARNO PRESS
A New York Times Company
New York — 1975

142706

Reprint Edition 1975 by Arno Press Inc.

Reprinted from a copy in
   The University of Illinois Library

The Italian American Experience
ISBN for complete set: 0-405-06390-3
See last pages of this volume for titles.

Manufactured in the United States of America

Library of Congress Cataloging in Publication Data

D'Agostino, Guido, 1910–
   Olives on the apple tree.

   (The Italian American experience)
   Reprint of the 1st ed. published by Doubleday, Doran,
New York.
   I. Title.   II. Series.
PZ3.D1350l9 ℂPS3507.A32꜕   813'.5'2   74-17924
ISBN 0-405-06397-0

OLIVES
ON
THE APPLE
TREE

GUIDO D'AGOSTINO

OLIVES
ON
THE APPLE
TREE

A NOVEL

NEW YORK
Doubleday, Doran & Company, Inc.
1940

PRINTED AT THE *Country Life Press*, GARDEN CITY, N. Y., U. S. A.

TO THE MEMORY OF MY FATHER

OLIVES
ON
THE APPLE
TREE

1

GIUSTINA GARDELLA found it a great satisfaction to live in the village and have her home situated where she could pause in her housework and glimpse the shabby life up on the hill from which she had saved her own family. For it was Giustina who decided, when the family first moved into the neighborhood, that they were not going to live with the poor Italians on Wop-Roost, but right down in the center of things where there was a chance to take advantage of opportunity and share in the prosperity of the New World.

Now, as Giustina stood by the window in the thickening night, her gaze fell away from the dull cluster of lights above and came to rest on the house directly across the street. Her lips pressed into a thin smile. She watched the illuminated sign out front as it slanted in the cold January wind. For the thousandth time since the sign had been placed there, almost a year back, she spelled out the glittering gold letters: Emile Gardella, M.D. Only, in reading, she could never get out of the habit of whispering Emilio to herself instead of the way the name appeared.

Behind her the dining-room table was set with the places ready and the wine gallon resting on the floor near the head. In an armchair in a corner of the room her husband sat with his hands folded over his stomach, waiting. Now and again he tugged at the massive gold chain across his vest to have a look at the time. He stared at his wife's back, ran his finger along the underpart of his huge mustache in a gesture of impatience and settled back in the armchair again.

Elena entered from the kitchen and stood near her mother at the window. She was much taller than her mother. Apart from the freshness, the glow of her youth, there was a grace of features, a tenderness of expression which, set against the gleaming frame of her ebony hair, produced an effect of quiet and enduring beauty. On the other hand, the mother shone cold and gave no feeling of warmth at all from behind her sharp cheekbones and small dark eyes and skin which had become the quality of unused leather. Elena cupped her hands and peered at the house across the street. "It's getting late. We had better start eating. Emilio can eat by himself when he gets in."

The mother shook her head. "We wait. Emilio be here now very soon. He no can be long."

Federico struggled his fat body out of the armchair and looked at his watch again. "What he do all this time? One lilla kids born. Is every day million kids born. No such a big job for doctor. Whyfor he gotta stay all day in the town?"

"What you know, you big stupid?"

"I know what I know. I know now is one years I pay all the bills for him. I know was maybe mistake he become doctor. Was better he no become nothing and help me with the bizaness. . . ."

"Who pay the bills?" Giustina shrieked.

Here Elena interrupted, "Stop arguing, for God sake." Then she added, "Anyway, Emilio oughtn't to stay away from his office so long. Giuseppe was down looking for him this afternoon. Nick hurt himself, or something. When people want a doctor they want him right away—not when the doctor gets good and ready to come."

The shrill blare of an automobile horn sounded outside. Giustina gave a hurried look through the window and rushed away to the kitchen. Federico took his place at the table. Mumbling under his breath, he lifted the gallon from the floor and poured a glass of wine. He tasted the wine without being able to make up his mind about it, tasted it again and then sat waiting for the food to appear.

Emilio entered the room. He tossed his coat over the back of his father's armchair, placed his hat on top of the coat and his gloves on top of the hat. He seemed to be in a good humor. He was smiling and it was the kind of smile which told everybody he was pleased with himself. As he sat down he rubbed his palms briskly together and winked at his sister. He picked up his napkin and dropped it carelessly into his lap in a manner which made him appear born to the part of the gentleman. And when he spoke, the voice came from his lips with the added flavor and confidence of his education.

"Christ, it's cold tonight," he said. "Thought the car would freeze standing outside the hospital all day."

Federico heard but he didn't answer. He sniffed the two broiled lamb chops and the spinach in his plate and began to eat slowly, now and then washing down the flavorless food with a mouthful of wine. Emilio shook his head. "With your liver the less you drink of that stuff the better you'll feel. I've told you that a million times. What's the use giving you any advice . . ."

"Look," Federico said. "I feel good. I feel fine. When I sick I call you. Now, shut up for the wine!"

Emilio ignored his father. He turned to his mother and said enthusiastically, "That Murphy baby! There was a piece of luck! An extremely difficult delivery. I worked like a horse. But this morning Doctor Stone came up to me and said, 'Excellent, my boy. You did a fine job on that case.' That's what he said."

"He big man at the hospital, no?" Giustina said proudly.

"I'll say. The chief of the whole works. You ought to see him. Tall. Distinguished. The real professional type. And the way he dresses! I'll bet every suit he got cost him over a hundred and fifty. There's my idea of a doctor. . . ."

"And he say you was a good doctor?" asking him to repeat for Federico's benefit. "It make me so happy. Tell you mamma everything."

"That's right," Emilio said, holding up his hands. "Here's what I got. I got the hands and I know how to use them. Don't you worry. I'll get my recognition yet. That's not the point. That'll come anyway. If only I could get in good with Stone and the crowd he runs around with I'd be sitting on top of the world. But these things don't just grow out of the air. Sure Stone thinks I'm a good doctor. But he's seen me around town a couple of times with Hazel Lambertson. And don't you believe that doesn't help. The money people—there you've got it. I hung around the hospital all afternoon just to have another talk with him. No shop talk. Oh no. Just hunting and the things he likes to talk about.

As Emilio paused for breath Elena said, "Giuseppe was looking for you. Nick hurt himself."

"I'll be up. I'll be up. A couple of things to attend to first. I've got an idea. Boy, if it only works!" His smile was shrewd and directed at his mother.

"But you can't neglect those who depend on you just because you want to work yourself into the social set in town. The poor people need doctors too."

Emilio threw down his napkin. He looked at the ceiling and drummed his fingers on the table. "Listen to her. Jesus Christ, ten years' hard study and work just to be doctor to a bunch of dumb wops! Not me. Damned if I will." He tried to reason with his sister. "How can a doctor practice good medicine with those greenhorns? They never have their prescriptions filled. They never take advice. No matter what you do they never appreciate it. Ever since I set up my shingle the only patients I've had are those goddamn Italians up on the hill and a few other poverty-stricken families around. The hell with that."

"Emilio, he right," Giustina said, rising to his defense. "Someday he be big doctor and live with high-class people. I say this from when he just start the school. I say this to you papa when I tell him, no, we no live up on the hill with Italiano people. Is here in the village we gotta live. You see now what we got!"

Federico raised his hand to say something and then let it fall. The effort was too great.

"That's just it," Elena said. "Here we are better off than anyone else around. I don't see what money has to do with it. I only see to be a good doctor and to take care of the sick regardless of their circumstances. That's what makes it wonderful to be a doctor. Without that a man might just as well become a plumber or a shoemaker."

Emilio ran his fingers through his hair, completely out of patience. His face became serious and his eyes acquired the same fierce determination expressive in his mother. "What's the use. This life is good enough for you. That's why you couldn't stay in college. That's why you came back here. Outside of fooling around with the old man's bookkeeping and collecting rents, you don't understand anything else. You'll wind up by marrying a plumber or a

shoemaker yourself one of these days. Go ahead, if that's
what you want. But not me. Damned if I'm going to remain
a little wop doctor in a one-jerk village all my life. I'll be
damned if I will. . . ."

Emilio left to go across the street to his own house, con-
sisting of his office and private living quarters. Elena helped
her mother with the dishes. Federico retired once more to
his armchair with a sigh, as though these dinner discussions
about ambition and the future wearied him. He had been
out in the cold all day long supervising the cutting of ice
on the mill pond and having it hauled to the icehouse, and
he felt tired. In the morning he expected Giuseppe, Tony
and Luca down from Wop-Roost to bury the thousand-
gallon tank for the new oil-burning system Giustina decided they must have in place of the old coal furnace.
Thinking of the frozen earth, the dull picks which he had
forgotten to take to the blacksmith, and picturing Luca
cursing his head off, he fell asleep.

A little later Giustina came and shook him roughly. He
yawned, stretched his arms lazily over his head and followed her upstairs to bed, pausing on the landing to wind
his heavy gold watch—a ritual to indicate the close of
another day.

In the living room, huddled in a corner of the sofa, Elena
sat reading and nibbling an apple. She finished the newspaper and started on the final chapter of a book she had

borrowed from the drugstore circulating library. Her mother called to her from upstairs, "Elena!"

"What?"

"No forget put out the light when you go to bed."

Elena didn't bother to answer. This was merely a part of the retiring process in the Gardella household.

Once, while she was reading, Elena got up and went to the window. There was a light in her brother's house and his car was outside, which meant he hadn't found time as yet to see what was the matter up on the hill. She knew it was nothing very serious, yet the thought of her brother being so callous troubled her. He hadn't always been this way. The change seemed to come somewhere between the time of going to college and serving his interneship in the city. College had done something to him, and the hospital had done something. And the past year with only a handful of patients and all of the poorer class had brought it out. He was becoming more and more calculating and hard.

A little later she got up and went to the closet in the hall for her coat. She didn't bother to put the coat on but pulled it about her shoulders tight, turning up the collar so that only the top of her head appeared in a black silky mound above the fur. She picked up her book and went out, closing the door gently behind her.

Crossing to her brother's house, the sweeping wind bundled her coat against her legs. She turned her back to the wind and hurried up the steps out of the cold. The door was open and the lights on in the waiting room, but Emilio was not at home. She stopped just long enough to survey the bright, modern furniture of chromium and Moroccan leather, and to allow the warmth of the room to remove a chill. A magazine lay carelessly thrown on the rug. She picked it up and set it on the table with the others, straightening the pile.

As she headed back across the street again, toward the frost-covered windows of the drugstore, the low group of commercial buildings further along seemed like an endless series of abandoned sheds, lifeless and bare in the deserted night. Beyond the drugstore the village had died, and suddenly the moon spread a ghostly pallor and the street became a twisted serpent's belly, stiff beneath her feet. Elena felt a shiver down her spine and quickened her footsteps.

In the drugstore she found Emilio huddled over the counter, deep in conversation with the druggist. She put down her book and proceeded to search through the score or so of titles on the shelves of the circulating library. Emilio glanced up at her and went right on talking.

"If only we could arrange it," he was saying to the druggist. "A crack at a nice big buck. He's one of those nuts on hunting. Give his right arm for a shot at a deer. Was telling me today he spent a week straight up in the mountains without even a smell of anything. Got so damn tired and cold he was almost ready to shoot the guide." He added slyly, "I checked up with Hazel Lambertson. The hell part of it is, over at the club all his friends came home with their buck. God, that burned him up."

The druggist slapped his thigh. He was a stubby man with a close crop of straw-colored hair and eyes like a bull-frog which appeared ready to pop out of his head whenever he laughed.

"I know that feeling all right. After a while you get so's you start shooting at chipmunks just to hear the gun go off."

"Chipmunks? Anything that moves in the brush. Told him I'd show him where he could pop off a deer right around here without driving a couple of hundred miles up to the mountains. You should have seen him look at me."

"What about the patient waiting for you up on the hill?" Elena asked suddenly.

"What was that?"

"Your patient. On the hill."

"Oh. Just let me finish what I'm doing here. Hell, this means more to me than all those wops up there put together."

"Yes, and I suppose Papa will pay the fine if the game warden catches you?"

Emilio struck his fist down on the counter. "Who said anything about getting caught? What's eating you anyway? Why don't you mind your own business and leave me alone?" He turned his back with a sullen shrug of his shoulders.

Elena picked out a book and sat down on one of the stools at the soda fountain. She ordered a hot chocolate. The druggist mixed a little cocoa with hot water and topped it off with a dash of whipped cream. He placed several sweet crackers in a plate to go with the order and then went back to Emilio as Elena sipped the steaming liquid and thumbed the pages of her book.

"Jesus," the druggist said, "the other day out rabbit hunting I saw deer tracks big as my two fists. Down in the swamp back of Wop-Roost. Musta been a buck the size of a horse. Remember, I told you about it."

"That's what I was thinking," Emilio said. "Bet he hangs out there in the swamp every night. Now they come down out of the mountains looking for food. Maybe Saturday? You and me and Doctor Stone. We'll cover the swamp and wait. We'll show him the damn biggest buck he ever saw. Drop it and leave it lay. Pick it up at night and hang it in the icehouse. That's the idea." He grinned and thumped the druggist on the chest with his fist. "Wait when I start sending you some fancy prescriptions in here to be filled. Boy, you just wait. It won't be long now."

The door opened slowly and a man walked in—a stranger. He was a lumbering brute nearly six feet tall with heavy shoulders. He looked around hesitantly at first. Then he saw the kerosene stove in the center of the room and walked up to it with arms outstretched to receive its heat. His hands were dry and cracked from the cold and he was dressed in a frayed black overcoat with a sweater underneath. The paper wrapping of some kind of package bulged out of his pocket. On his feet he wore heavy laborer's shoes and on his head a dirty gray cap pulled down over his ears. The druggist immediately sprang from behind the counter.

"What do you want?"

The man pressed closer to the stove. He was young, somewhere in his early thirties. He looked at the druggist and then mumbled politely, "I do not think you will mind if I make myself warm?"

The druggist appeared suspicious. He didn't know what to answer. Emilio came over, attracted by the voice. He studied the stranger from head to foot, allowing his gaze to linger on the swarthy complexion. "Jesus Christ, another Italian!"

The man smiled, his teeth straight and perfect and gleaming. "Si. And you too," he said.

Emilio changed color. "What's that got to do with anything?" However, he asked in a voice which seemed to indicate that he owned the drugstore and everything in it, including the stove which gave so freely of its warmth to the vagrant, "Where do you come from?"

The man raised his hand in an indefinite gesture. "The highway. I see the lights here of the village."

"Devil with him," the druggist said, taking Emilio's arm and drawing him away. "Let him get warm." He bent over and in a low voice continued to plan the details of the deer hunt.

Elena kept her back turned to the stranger. In the mirror behind the soda fountain she could see him. He was watching her. His eyes were on her back and she could feel them.

She raised the cup to her lips to finish what was left of the chocolate. Over the top of the cup she saw him in the mirror and followed his eyes and then she knew. It wasn't her back the man was watching but her cup and the plate at her elbow with the two crackers. She suddenly became embarrassed, confused, and the color rushed to her cheeks. She slid off the stool with the book under her arm and moved quickly through the door.

When she had gone the vagrant edged closer to the soda fountain. He kept his eyes on Emilio and the druggist, and when he thought they weren't looking picked up one of the crackers. Emilio saw him.

"Of all the damn nerve!"

Now the druggist went toward the fellow. He was angry. He said to Emilio, "That's the trouble. You be nice. You give these fellows a break and before you know it they're walking off with the whole store."

"You're right. I've seen it again and again over at the Swan Inn," Emilio said. "I used to think different. They want a cup of coffee. Then it's a sandwich. Then a couple of sandwiches for the next day. So long as they got a bite to eat they don't give a damn about anything else. Work? Like hell. You couldn't get one of these guys to work for the love of money. Just bums off the road. They live and die on the road—I know."

The man looked straight at Emilio. There was mockery in his eyes as he regarded the tender shaven face, the immaculate clothing and the delicate hands which had never known the hurting power of cold.

"It is easy for you to talk like that when you have your stomach full," he said. "What do you know about work, you?"

The druggist backed away to get behind the counter where he always kept a club ready for such emergencies. The vagrant watched him and put his hand on the doorknob. Emilio clenched his fists. He saw the druggist was ready.

"Go on, beat it!"

The man lingered a moment and then pulled the door open. But before he could turn to go out a figure brushed past him into the store. It was Giuseppe from Wop-Roost looking for Emilio.

Giuseppe went up to Emilio, his hands spread helplessly and his mouth twisted into an expression of deep concern. He was a little bit of a man with a pinched face which stuck out from the flaps of his hunting cap like a woodchuck peeping from its hole. He wore a tattered hunting coat and canvas breeches and heavy felt boots with arctics over them, so that when he walked it sounded as if a giant was coming along.

"Please, Doctor Emilio," he pleaded, "you come? Nick, he raise hell with the leg. He holler like a bull. Angelina, she go crazy. He make everybody crazy up there."

"In a couple of minutes," Emilio said. His eyes were still fixed on the vagrant who stood in the doorway watching

Giuseppe. The man raised his head. Emilio's glance never wavered. His jaws were set. As the man went out Emilio's features relaxed and he broke into a grin. He turned to Giuseppe. "What's all the excitement about anyway?"

"Dio mio!" Giuseppe said, bringing his palms together. "That crazy Nick. Alla time he walk with his head up in the air like he smell something dirty. Today he go for to see about one job prune some trees and he slip on the road and fall down. Was no so bad first. Then begin to hurt. Now he holler like he was dead. Jeasuma Christ, whyfor that man no can watch where he walk?"

"Where is the injury?"

"Huh? Oh." Giuseppe brought his leg up and pounded his knee. "Is here. Is right here where is the hurt."

"Probably nothing much," Emilio said. "Anything in the knee hurts like hell. I'll go over and get my bag and be up in a little while."

"Please—you no forget? If you no come, is nobody sleep tonight."

"I said I'd come, didn't I?"

Giuseppe was afraid to press Emilio further. He drew the collar of his hunting coat tight about his neck and went out. The druggist came from behind the counter, still gripping the upper half of a pick handle. He flourished it in the air a few times for a bit of practice. Emilio laughed. He dug his hands in his pockets and shook his head. He couldn't get over the hobo.

"Imagine that bastard!" he said.

GIUSEPPE bent low with the wind and headed toward the dirt road leading up to Wop-Roost. He was thinking of his troubles, the brutal cold, and cursing under his breath when he heard a footstep beside him and felt someone touch his arm. He sprang around quickly. Recognizing the figure of the man he had seen in the drugstore, he said angrily, "Whatsamatter? You crazy, scare me like this?"

"Scusate."

"Watch you wants?"

"I see you in the drugstore," the vagrant said in a voice filled with apology. "You are an Italian like me. Maybe you will tell me where I can find a place to sleep—maybe something to eat?"

Giuseppe leaned closer to have a good look at the man. "You broke?" he asked.

There was no answer.

"You bum?"

The man raised his hand and let it fall. Giuseppe fought with himself for a second. Then he said in a quick, unnatural voice, "Is no use. I sorry. Now I got too much trooble. Is Nick, the brother from my wife before she die. He live with me now. He broke too. Is my lilla Angelina. She complain alla time. The house she is no more like a house—is like a stable. Is regular wop house like live Tony and Beppo and Luca. No use. I no can help you."

Giuseppe walked off, leaving the vagrant standing in the middle of the street. A little further on he turned and yelled, "Is over there one barn. You go in there and you no be too cold."

The man stood motionless with his shoulders hunched and watching Giuseppe until his darkening form merged with the night. His mouth opened and he uttered one word, "L'America!"

He made his way slowly toward the hulking silhouette of the barn in a vacant lot some distance away. It was an old building, crooked on its foundation, and had been used for many years without repair as a shelter for lumber. The boards had spread apart in places and there were cracks where the wind roared through. He entered and struggled to close the door after him. It remained open, showing a wide gap into the night, creaking and groaning on rusty hinges.

He walked around the empty structure in the darkness,

feeling, groping for a place out of the wind. Everywhere he moved there was the cutting chill at his back, on his chest, slashing his entire body. His feet became numb. He sat down on the ground, taking off his shoes one at a time, rubbing his feet with his hands and massaging the tips of his toes which were sticking through holes in his socks. Then the numbness began to creep into his thighs and into his buttocks and he got up, running about the barn, slapping his arms and jouncing his legs.

He huddled in a corner shivering and hitting his hands against the side of the wall until tears came into his eyes. Then, through a knothole, he saw the lighted windows of the drugstore. The light blurred and danced, came closer, tantalizing. Behind the light there was warmth, the oilstove with its radiating heat, its soft heat, its wonderful heat. Then figures loomed in front of the stove, giants with their arms folded, laughing at him and mocking. He reached out and fumbled in the darkness. Something hard and round came into his grasp. It was a piece of pipe used for rolling lumber. He clutched it in both hands just as a voice called, "Hey, Meesta Bum!"

He staggered up the hill, half frozen, mutely following the bobbing little figure of Giuseppe. Giuseppe tried to explain. He clicked his tongue several times. "I come all the way here and then I stop. Sangue di Cristo, Giuseppe! You leave there one man to freeze. Italiano too. In you house you got fire, you got bread. What you care when you warm and you got you belly full? Go to hell, everybody else. But is no Giuseppe, this. Is no Giuseppe leave even a dog cold and without eat. Is no Giuseppe be afraid be boss in his house."

Now the shacks of Wop-Roost began to gather form, group in shadows against the sky. Here and there a window threw dull light upon the outer world—the woodpile, discarded wine barrels, endless accumulated rubbish of no particular use.

Giuseppe led the way to a shack standing apart from the others. As they approached close, a hound-dog, hearing unfamiliar footsteps along with those of his master, sprang forward with a growl. "Go sleep!" Giuseppe commanded, and the dog turned and went nosing through the burlap flap covering the mouth of his kennel. Giuseppe watched the shivering flanks disappear.

"Where that salamambitch doctor?" a voice called as they entered the shack. Giuseppe paid no attention. He grabbed a chair and pulled it close to the potbelly stove glowing red in the center of the room.

"Here. You sit down. You get warm," he said to the vagrant.

The door leading to another room opened and a girl came out. She was about seventeen, with a lovely mass of chestnut hair falling to her shoulders and a schoolgirl's innocence of face. She was smiling in confusion, and her lips showed the fresh touch of lipstick. When she saw the stranger she glanced hurriedly about the room, looking for someone else. Then suddenly the brightness was gone from her world.

Giuseppe went up to her and began to whisper excitedly, "What I gonna do? Poor fellow was freeze and hongry. What I was gonna do?"

The girl's mouth became firm. She turned and went back into her room. Giuseppe followed—arguing, pleading. He kicked the door shut with his heel. Still his voice could be heard, a muffled undertone through the flimsy partition mingling with the groaning and cursing of the ailing man lying on the couch.

The vagrant sat huddled over, shivering. His face and hands changed to a lobster-red from the heat of the roaring fire. He listened to the insistent mumbling at his back, "Santa Madonna, miseria! All afternoon. All afternoon. Is poor wop could die before he come!" He shifted the chair around and said, "He will be here in a little while, the doctor."

Nick pulled himself up from under the covers to a sitting position on the couch. His red bulbous face twisted in pain at the exertion. He stared at the vagrant, somewhat puzzled, forgetting momentarily about the pain in his leg. "Who you? Where you come from?"

"My name is—Marco. Who am I?" The man shrugged. "Just that I have no money and I am on the road. But I hear the doctor say he will be here very soon now."

Nick laughed sarcastically. "He be here soon! If was somebody from the town he be here in one minuts. But no, because is up here he no give a damn. What the hell he gonna be big doctor take care Italiano people? He want nice people, rich people. But is no so easy like that—like he think, like his mamma think. I tell you, when people is get lilla money they forget where they come. They think right away they high class too. Just for Elena, is one salamam-bitch family the whole bunch down there."

Giuseppe barged into the room again. He shouted at Nick. "Shut up you face. Whyfor you gotta break every-body head with you talk? Doctor Emilio he very busy all day. He say he come right away."

Now the girl stood in the doorway eying her uncle de-fiantly. Her lips trembled and she was about to say some-thing, but Giuseppe took her arm and urged her to the kitchen. "Please, Angelina!" he begged, "the man he hongry. You get him something like a good girl."

Angelina came out of the kitchen with a loaf of bread, some dry, hard cheese and some olives. She set everything on the table and then vanished into her room again. Marco began to eat, tearing off chunks of bread with his hands, biting into the cheese and swallowing faster than he could chew. Both Giuseppe and Nick looked on in amazement.

"Jeasuma Christ, was no joke you was hongry," Giuseppe said. He got down on his knees and pulled a jug of wine out from under the couch where Nick was lying. He filled a water glass with wine and handed it to the vagrant. "Is my own wine; I make from my own grapes. No too bad. You taste youself."

Marco raised the glass. He started to drink and kept drinking in long, steady gulps until the glass was empty. He set the glass down on the table. He held his face lowered and seemed to be looking into his lap. Giuseppe waited for a verdict on the wine. Then he saw the man's head lift and saw the smile trying to force itself upon his lips.

A few minutes later the dog barked and there came the sound of an automobile approaching. First the dogs down at the other shacks began barking and then Giuseppe's dog. Giuseppe called to his daughter, "Angelina! Angelina!" To Nick he said, "Please, you keep you big mouth close. What you think or no thing, just the same I get plenty work from family Gardella. Is no use starve because you think everybody from down below no good."

Emilio entered and set down his black leather bag. He started to take off his gloves with a professional brusqueness, intent only on the work before him and Angela smiling in the background. He saw the man sitting at the table without really seeing him. Then he paused suddenly with the fingers of one hand pulling at the thumb of his glove on the other.

"Well I'll be——"

Angela came over and took his coat. She hung it on a nail near the door. Now Emilio recovered from his surprise and his manner became sure and confident again. He winked at Angela. Nick called from the couch, "Is about

time you get here. How you know maybe I no die wait for
you?"

"I wouldn't worry about that. Come on, let's have a look
at that leg."

Nick threw the covers aside, keeping a corner of the
blanket to cover his middle. His cheeks puffed and he bit
into his lip as he reached to pull up his underwear. The
knee was swollen and inflamed and had turned blue just
below the kneecap. Emilio's eyes followed down Nick's leg
to his foot. "You might try washing your feet once in a
while," he said.

"Whatsamatter, my feet? Is lilla bit dirty? Is same kind
of feet what you got. You forget is same kind of feet work
with you papa in the ditch before he make money and send
you to school."

Emilio grinned. He was used to this kind of talk from
Nick. Giuseppe and Angela were more embarrassed than
he was. Only he could not be rid of the uncomfortable
sensation of the other man watching at his back and listening. He bent over to examine the knee, feeling, touching
his finger here and there about the inflamed area. He
gripped the kneecap firmly and worked it in a slow circular
motion.

"Aiee!" Nick hollered.

"Keep quiet. It doesn't hurt that much."

"Bestia! Is my leg. How you know how my leg hurt?"

"Because I know."

Emilio concluded his diagnosis. "Slight patella fracture

and a torn ligament. Have to bind it up." He went over to his bag resting on a chair near the table and pulled out a roll of adhesive tape. Now the hobo was smiling. "What are you smiling at?" he asked sullenly.

"I was thinking how wonderful it is to be the doctor. To help people that suffer. That is what I was thinking and it makes me feel good."

"Jesus Christ," Emilio mumbled through his teeth.

When he had finished a tight binding of tape about Nick's knee he asked Angela if he could wash his hands and followed her into the little partitioned-off section at the end of the room used for a kitchen. Marco could see them through the open doorway. He saw Emilio bend to Angela as she worked the handle of the pump over the sink and whisper something into her ear. He saw Angela nod her head and smile shyly.

Giuseppe hurried to fill a clean glass with wine. He held it, waiting as Emilio came out of the kitchen. "You have a drink. Is good for the cold. Make you feel warm when you go outside."

Emilio shook his head. "Thanks."

"Is wine I make myself. Is good. Come on, I have a drink too."

"I don't like wine," Emilio said. And to Nick, "Better not try to use that leg for a while. Just lie in bed and take it easy. I'll be up again in a couple of days."

Giuseppe still held the glass in his hand, almost insisting on Emilio drinking with him, but he caught his daughter's glance and lowered the glass away. He fumbled into his pocket for his purse and painstakingly counted out three dollars and handed them over.

When the purring of Emilio's car died away down the road to the village Giuseppe sent Angela to bed. He divided the full glass of wine into three equal portions and sat down a little longer. He threw some more wood into the stove and cleared a place in the center of the floor. "Is no bed. But here on the floor you be all right. Last years I make foundation all around so the wind no blow under. You keep the fire and you be fine."

"It is not the first time I sleep on the floor," Marco said. He laughed, thinking of some of the nights he had spent when there wasn't even a floor or a stove. And the stinking, smelly nights huddled together with fifty or sixty others like himself in a single room, and in the morning the vile coffee and the false gratitude and thanks, which was the hardest part of all.

Giuseppe took a swallow of wine and rubbed his chin pensively. He leaned forward with his arms on his knees, watching the glowing metal of the stove and the little ridges of dust which formed millions of tiny sparks— wiped out one minute, appearing again the next.

"Is no my bizaness," he said. "But many times I see somebody like you and I think, whyfor this man gotta move alla time? Whyfor he no can stand still like other people? Me, I be here twenty years now. I have my wife and she die. I have my lilla girl and she grow up. But always I be here. Is home. Is this house what I call my house. Is my garden. Is my chickens. Is my dog and the hunting with my friends. Whyfor I gonna go someplace where is not sure what I find?"

Marco was a long time answering. Giuseppe raised a shoulder. "I just ask to know, that's all. You Italiano like me, and with you I can talk. Whyfor nice young fellow be bum when could have nice life with wife and kids and place to live?"

"Because," Marco said. He started to speak slowly, weighing his words, trying to fit them into their proper place. "Because I have been here now for six, seven years. I have seen this country from bottom to top. I have worked at every kind of job and I have found nothing to make me stay in one place. I see one big goddamn country—rich, beautiful, like never I have seen anything before and all I feel is I want to keep moving. Everybody I find like your doctor here, and Nick over there—mad, sore like hell about something. Nobody satisfied with anything, and I have become so that I sick myself with this American sickness."

Marco rose from his chair. He looked at Giuseppe, his jaw set and his eyes a trifle wild. He clenched his fist.

"Always I have looked for people like me—Italians. I have looked for the love of the things that I love because I am me and my father was my father. Is something inside goes 'way, 'way back. The love of the work and what you do. The love of the ground and the good crops. The love of the grapes and the good wine. The love of the food and the table and the conversation, the laughing and everything else that makes the life worth while. I was so sure to find all this here. Better than over there, because here the man is free and can do what he wants and say what he wants—and the country so big and so rich, with plenty for everybody."

"Is here," Giuseppe said. "Is here I have found a good life with my friends—with Tony and Luca and Beppo and Vincenzo and everybody else. We no rich but we work and we eat. For me is fine. Only for Angelina I think maybe sometime was better if I have more money and no live so much with Italiano people."

Nick raised on his elbow and swallowed the remainder of the wine in his glass. He scowled at Giuseppe. "Is here I find every salamambitch for what I work give it to me—you know where." He directed his voice at Marco. "I have my wife and my kids and I think I doing fine. Seven years one job take care of farm with house for myself and everything nice. Then I say to the boss, 'Boss, is plenty money now to be make in peaches. I clear for you fifteen acres bad land and plant peaches and we split.' Three years I work like a horse—night, Sunday, after I finish work on the farm. I clear the land. I plant the trees. I take care. Then the state come. So much land for the new highway and picnic place. The boss sell out. My peaches for what I work? Go to hell me and my work. Is good country for you, Giuseppe. For me is fulla crap. My family go back and I am here all alone, make five, ten dollar every week—one lilla job here, on lilla job there. . . ."

"And that is America," Marco said vehemently. "Everything is all mixed up. The farmer is no more farmer, he has become the businessman. The man who was good to handle stone, now he is a slave in the laundry. Is no more the work, but the money makes the man different one from the other. I look for the Italian. What I have found? No more the Italian but a bastard Italian. Quick he forgets everything from the old country to make money and have a car and buy food in cans and become just like the American he is working for. But he does not become the American and he is no more the Italian. Something in the middle —no good for himself and no good for the country. A real bastardo!"

As Marco raised his voice Giuseppe grew proportionately uneasy. Somehow the argument was getting into channels over his head, and there was something fierce, rebellious in this stranger's voice which frightened him. He talked a little bit like Nick when Nick grew real excited, only much worse and with more intelligence, and this made Giuseppe all the more uneasy. He was grateful no one from down below was present to listen. Now Marco walked over to Nick and tapped him on the shoulder.

"I will tell you something funny—you, farmer, mad because somebody cheated you from your money. Do you know on what I worked when I first came here? Was a fellow said to me, 'You want to make money? Okay, you make money like me—shine shoes.' For six months I lived with him in one room with his family in the city with the houses one on top of the other and every day I shine shoes for him in his place. Me, shine shoes! Me, who when I was just a little kid I helped my brothers in the vineyards. Me, who comes from a family where the land and the work of the land is in the blood from the time before anybody knows. Shine shoes! Day after day after day for every louse who has ten cents to pay and can talk with a cigar in his mouth and say, 'Hurry up! Wop! Greenhorn! Pasta-fasool!' "

Nick laughed. He thought it was a funny joke. He shook his head. "I see one time in the city a friend from me who have a shoeshine place just like you say. 'Jeasuma Christ, Joe. How you live such a bastich life?' He raise his head and he raise his hands like this. 'What I gonna do?' he say. 'Is no no more me, is the kids. Like this I give them to eat and I send them to school so they grow up and no have to do what I do.' "

"But that is not the worst, shining shoes," Marco added quickly. "I told it go to hell before I starved. I found some-body knows my family from a long time. In the dress busi-ness he was, with a big car and plenty of money. So I go to work in the dress business. For one year I worked—wrap boxes, throw the boxes on the truck, push the wagon with the dresses all around the city. It was not so bad. I was here. I was there. Anyway, I was moving. But I could not make more than ten dollars. How can I live with ten dollars? I talked to the boss and he said, 'Marco, is only one way to make money in this business. It is to learn the machine—the sewing machine.'"

Marco paused. He looked first at Nick then at Giuseppe. Giuseppe tried to appear disinterested. He gazed at the wall, at the floor and at the ceiling. Nevertheless, his body inclined forward as Marco said, "Do you know what it is, the sewing machine?"

"Sure," Nick said. "What you talk? Everybody know what is a sewing machine."

"Well, that is what I learned, and that is how I worked—on the sewing machine! Not me alone. Maybe twenty men just like me and we worked in a line with the women, on the sewing machine. Big fellows! Good for the field and the hard work. All day long behind the needle, making dresses just like little girls. That is what I learned! That is how I worked—on the lousy, sonofabitch of a sewing machine until I thought I would go crazy, or kill somebody."

Marco paced back and forth across the floor. He seemed set to go on talking indefinitely. Then he saw the concern in Giuseppe's face and became calm. He smiled and unbuttoned his sweater. "I am sorry. I did not mean to talk so much. But it is such a long time I have no one to listen that I forget. And maybe I have been too long hungry and cold. That has something to do with it too."

"Is all right," Giuseppe said because he couldn't think of anything else to say. "But now is late and is better we sleep."

He got up and yawned. He went into his own room for a minute, a little cubbyhole squeezed between Angela's room and the kitchen, and came out with a heavy army blanket which he spread on the floor. He looked at the fire, threw in a few more short logs from a pile in the corner and turned the damper low. Then he reached for his hunting coat. "You have to come outside first?"

Marco nodded. He buttoned his sweater again and followed Giuseppe through the door. As they stood against the building with their backs humped and their faces turned away from the wind the dog came over and sniffed at Marco's legs. He reached down and scratched the dog's head.

"Poor bastich," Giuseppe said. "Is too cold tonight for to sleep in the barrel. Maybe I let him in for lilla while. Watch you think?"

"You ask me?"

Inside again, Giuseppe grabbed the dog by the collar and made him lie down near the stove. He said to Marco in a whisper, "Please. When comes the morning, you put him out. If Angelina see, she raise hell."

At the door to his room he hesitated, somewhat embarrassed, looking across from Marco to his shotgun standing against the wall. He went over and picked it up, at the same time making a feeble attempt to explain. "Is in case the fox come for the chickens. I keep the gun ready and I shoot him from the window."

Marco smiled. He unlaced his shoes and took off his

sweater, rolling it into a ball for a pillow. Next he pulled the bulging package from the pocket of his overcoat and unwrapped it. It contained two heavy work shirts, shaving equipment, several handkerchiefs and a pair of socks—clean but in worse condition than those he was wearing. He placed his possessions on a chair and then switched off the electric bulb hanging on a long wire from the ceiling. In the darkness he slipped off his shoes and stretched out on the blanket, wrapping it snug about him and pulling his coat over the top.

From the stove narrow slits of light played across the floor and upon the unpainted composition board of the walls and ceiling. Behind the door facing him he heard Giuseppe turn in bed and the springs creak. For a little while there was only the crackling silence of the fire. But he could feel, and he knew, that Nick was awake—watching him. The dog raised on his haunches and thumped at his neck with his hind foot. He opened his jaws in a silly yawn and flopped down again with a sigh. Marco reached over and stroked the dog's muzzle. Nick coughed a couple of times. Then he groaned and twisted his leg over to a sleeping position.

Down in the village Elena sat in the living room trying to concentrate on the pages of the book before her. The heat from the banked furnace had dwindled away and she sat huddled on the couch with her mother's knitted shawl about her shoulders and her feet pulled up under her skirt.

Her eyelids drooped, her head swayed and the book tilted in her hands. She wanted to go upstairs to bed, yet she waited on.

At last she heard Emilio's car pull into the driveway. She got up quickly and went through the hall to the kitchen, switching on the light over the back stoop. She placed a kettle of water on the stove and rubbed her palm over the frosted windowpane, watching her brother slide the heavy garage doors shut. As he returned past the house she edged the door open a crack and called to him.

"What's the matter with the old man, leaving that oil tank sticking out in the middle of the drive?" Emilio said upon entering the kitchen. "I damn near smacked into it as I came through." He glanced up at the white enamel clock over the stove. "What are you doing up so late anyway?"

"I was reading. Now I'm having a cup of tea. Want some?"

"That's an idea. Pour me a cup."

Elena turned the gas high under the kettle. She watched the water come to a boil and dropped in the tea leaves. She placed two cups on the table and Emilio sat down. He didn't bother to take his coat off. "You know," he said as Elena poured the tea. "At the hospital everybody gets into the habit of calling you by your last name. Hey, Gardella, they say. Makes me feel like a wop greenhorn."

"Now don't harp on that again."

"I don't care what the old man says. He should have

listened to Mamma and changed it a long time ago. Gardell.
That's the way it ought to be. Doctor Emile Gardell. But
you can bet your boots if I ever get out of this stinking
village, or open an office in town, I'll change it, yes sir."

"Drink your tea," Elena said. "Do you mean to tell me
you were up on the hill all this time?"

"Oh no. After I got through up there I stopped at the
drugstore again." He took a sip of tea and smiled. "God,
that Nick is funny sometimes. Did he squawk when I
probed around his knee. Just a torn ligament, but you'd
have thought I was going to amputate. Now there's a funny
thing about Italians. They can't seem to stand pain much.
The least scratch and they're all shot to pieces. But what
gets me about those shacks up there is the whiff when you
enter—you know, that closed-in smell as if there'd been
no ventilation for years, that mixture of body odor, sour
wine, cheese and garlic. Christ, it gags you. Giuseppe's place
isn't so bad. At least you can walk around without tripping
over somebody's boots, or a dog, or a gallon of wine.
Angela's responsible for that, I guess. You know, only the
past month or so I've been noticing how that kid has de-
veloped. Just since she finished high school. Not bad."
Emilio accented approval by a lift of his eyebrows.

"Falling back on yourself, aren't you?" Elena laughed.

"Not me. I've got a different kind of fish to fry. You saw
my meat that night at the hospital benefit ball." Emilio
nodded with satisfaction. "Hazel Lambertson, daughter of
one of the best lawyers in town. Blonde. Finishing school.

Picture in the local society columns. Yes sir, don't you worry about your big brother getting along. But Angela? What's the harm being nice to the girl? Suppose I do take her to the movies or out for a ride in the car once in a while? What the hell, a guy has to do something to pass the time in this lousy village."

"Something to pass the time," Elena mimicked. "If you don't watch out, one of these fine nights you're liable to find yourself passing the time with a stiletto between your ribs."

"Go on! That's in the story books. That was in Sicily a hundred years ago. Wake up, girlie! This is the good old U. S. You don't knife a man because he necks your daughter. You knife him if he don't."

Elena rose to clear the table. As Emilio prepared to go she asked in an offhand manner, "By the way, what happened to that hobo who was in the drugstore tonight?"

"What makes you ask?"

"Oh, just wondering."

"Because I almost belted the bastard," Emilio said. "Tried to pull a fast one. Walked over to the counter and picked up a couple of crackers as if he owned the place. Then the next thing I know I find him up at Giuseppe's shack. There he was, sitting at the table, eating and drinking and acting as unconcerned as you please. The fool Giuseppe took him in. But there's something about that guy I don't like. I can't figure it out. He annoys me. He gets under my skin."

JUST as morning broke Marco shivered and opened his eyes. The fire was out and the gray light of dawn gave the room a bare, unpleasant feeling. But the wind had died. He listened. The wind was dead. And this in itself was something to smile about.

In another minute he was up, arching his back, working his arms back and forth. He unrolled his sweater and put it on quickly. Then he folded the blanket out of the way and proceeded to fuss with the stove, poking in paper and wood, watching the flames kindle. The dog sat at his feet, interested, slapping his tail from side to side and jerking his head into comical angles. Over on the couch Nick grunted and rolled the phlegm in the back of his throat. He heard Giuseppe getting out of bed. Making a soft, clicking sound with his tongue, he called the dog to the front door.

As he greeted the clear morning sky he noted with surprise a thin layer of fresh-fallen snow. He followed the dog outside. The snow crunched underfoot. It formed breathless little ridges on the twigs and branches of the trees. He walked away from the house a short distance in the footprints of the dog who ran ahead, playfully burying his nose in the snow and snorting at the scent of a field mouse.

Now the shacks of Wop-Roost reached out in an irregular pattern before his eyes. The large shacks and the small shacks, most of them covered with tar paper held in place by lathing strips evenly spaced in a series of vertical lines as if patient for the plasterer's trowl and the stucco which never seemed to arrive.

But there was life, and sound, and movement, an air of living in this little hilltop community of his own people. Here and there the yellow smoke of a rekindled fire in the cookstove curled lazily upward. From crude shelter adjacent to each dwelling came the cackling of chickens, the bleating of goats and the grunting of hungry pigs. A door opened and a bucket of water sloshed out, leaving a dark stain across the bright surface of the snow. A baby started to wail and a dog barked. An angry masculine voice shouted something in Italian. It was the beginning of a new day on Wop-Roost.

Giuseppe waved from the house and walked over. He stood beside Marco with his hunting cap pushed back on his head and grinning as he struggled with his shirttail.

Marco took in the entire countryside with a sweep of his hand. "The land is beautiful here with the hills all around and over there the lake. It makes a picture I remember from home."

"Is beautiful all right," Giuseppe agreed. "Sometimes I think is better live up here than down there. Up here is everything open and you see with you eyes the whole world. You look and is never the same. Always change and become different. And no cost nothing. But you come with me and I show you something. Then after we eat, because today I got to go to work." He cupped his hands over his mouth and shouted, "Hey, Tony!"

The window of a shack further along opened and a man stuck his head out.

"Ho?"

"You pass by here when you ready? You get Luca?"

"Okay," Tony said and closed the window.

Giuseppe first went into the house for a pail of water and then led Marco around to the chicken coop. He opened the door and a dozen or so large white chickens fluttered to greet him. "Is no a nice bunch of chicken?" proudly. "Is called White—White—I forget the name, but is no Leghorn. Is too big chicken for that. Cluck! Cluck! I raise myself from lilla chicks one day old what I buy in the feed store."

He went inside and scooped a couple of handfuls of corn from a covered butter tub, scattered it over the floor, listening to the ringing clatter of beaks. He examined the hopper to see if there was enough mash for the day. Then he broke the ice out of the water pan and filled it again.

"How many eggs do you get?"

Giuseppe shook his head. "Is not so many like I expect. Is fourteen chicken and I get maybe four, five eggs. Is no too good. But is some nice bunch chicken just the same."

Marco entered the coop and closed the door. He reached down quickly and grabbed up a chicken, holding it cackling under his arm while he made a thorough examination of the comb, the feet, the pelvic bones and the vent. He set the chicken loose and then turned to Giuseppe. "You see that chicken, and this one and this one? One, two, three, four. Chop the heads off. They will never lay, those chickens. Just eat and cost you money and produce nothing. It is like when a man pays you to work. When you do not work he will not pay you—right?"

Giuseppe turned his palms upward.

"Good. Why then pay the chicken with food when she does not work? It is not good business. You will go broke. So, when you raise chickens, you must keep only the chickens that lay and all the rest you eat. Like that you have a profit for what you spend. Like that you do not throw your money away."

Giuseppe dug his hands into his back pockets. "Jeasuma Christ, I never think of it like that before. Is why the chicken cost me so much for feed." He raised the side of his shoe and aimed a kick. "Go to hell, bastich chicken what eat and no work. Tonight I chop you head off."

As Giuseppe locked the door of the chicken coop Marco explained how it was possible to tell the difference between a layer and a cull by the coloration of the feet and the comb, the space between the pelvic bones and the appearance of the vent.

"I hear that before," Giuseppe said, "but I have nobody to show me. In the book from the feed it tell. Many times I ask Angelina to read what the book say, but she no like to read about chicken. Sometime I wonder what the hell good is the school. If was me, I read all about things like this and I know everything. But for a girl is differenza, I guess. Is to have good time. Is to find good husband with plenty money so no have to live up on the hill with poor Italiano people."

When they entered the house Nick was sitting up on the couch. Giuseppe called, "Ho, Nicolo! How you feel today? You feel fine with the leg?"

"I feel is one chance I got to make ten dollar and I no can leave the house. That's what I feel."

"Is all right," Giuseppe said. "In couple days you be all fix like Doctor Emilio say and you find plenty work on the trees. For now you take it easy. But next time you keep you face where the ground go, because if you break you neck I got no money for the box and the hole."

This latter thought appealed to Giuseppe's sense of humor and he laughed. He went over to the door of his daughter's room and knocked loudly. "Angelina! Angelina! Is late now. If you go to the town to look for job, is time to get up. The job no wait for you, you know."

"I'm getting up," Angelina called, her voice drawling out of a deep sleep and fading back into it again.

The coffee pot setting on top of the stove was boiling. Giuseppe dumped in the coffee and removed the pot, placing it on the table. Next he lifted the iron lid from the stove and slid a frying pan over the hole, cracked several eggs into it and threw the shells into the fire. As the odor of cooking permeated the room Angela's voice rang out, "Are you cooking in the living room again?"

"I got no time to fool with the kerosene," Giuseppe shouted. "If you no like you get up youself and cook my breakfoist. Is too bad you no can cook for you papa when he got to go to work."

"Good God!"

"Good God, youself!"

Marco gathered his things off the chair and wrapped them into a package again. He stuffed the package into the pocket of his overcoat and slung the coat over his shoulder.

"Giuseppe!" Nick cried from the couch.

"Whatsamatter?" Giuseppe said. "Whyfor you put on you coat? Where you go?"

"Now you have done enough," Marco answered. "Last night you gave me food. You gave me wine and a place to sleep. I thank you very much. But I can take no more."

Giuseppe grabbed Marco's coat and hung it on the wall.
"If you go without eat, I be mad. I swear; I be offend. I
think you no like my house and what I got to eat. I am
right, Nick?"

"Sure you right. In my house I be offend too."

There was no use to argue. Marco removed his cap once
more. Nick sat up on the edge of the couch. He wrapped
himself in a blanket and Marco and Giuseppe gave him a
hand as he hopped across the room with his injured leg stiff
out before him. He eased into a chair and pulled another
over to rest his leg on. "Is a terrible life," he grunted. "Alla
time I got something. If is no from one thing is from another. Jeasuma Christ Almighty!"

While they were eating, Tony came in. He was dressed
much like Giuseppe, a hunting coat over several sweaters,
brown hunting cap and canvas breeches which hung down
around his hips. He stomped the snow from his boots and
greeted everybody without bothering to take his corn cob
pipe from his mouth. He looked at Marco and nodded. He
kidded Nick. "Ho, Bellagamba! How you today? I think
is just excuse, the leg, so you no have to work—yes?" He
pushed Nick's shoulder.

"Where Luca?" Giuseppe asked.

Tony took the pipe from between his teeth and put it
down on the table. He yanked the door of the stove open
and spit into the fire. "Luca no work today. He go hunt
rabbits with Beppo."

"Whatsamatter him?" Giuseppe said in exasperation.

"Yesterday when Meesta Gardella ask for three men to bury the tank Luca he say, fine, he come. He crazy sometimes, I think."

"Was yesterday. Yesterday was freeze weather. He think today be same. But when he see the sun and the snow and no more wind: go to hell Meesta Gardella—Whyfor he want to work? He go hunt rabbits with Beppo."

"Sure. Sure. I onderstand. Is nobody like hunt better from me. But when is time to work, is no time for hunt. Tomorrow maybe I go myself. But no today when I say I be on the job."

"Luca do good last years," Tony said with a note of envy in his voice. "He dig four wells, one hundred fifty buck each one. He have plenty to eat—plenty macaroni and plenty wine. He no have to worry for the kids. Betchamylife, if the ice bizaness be so good for me I tell Meesta Gardella go to hell myself today." He looked through the window at the sun creeping up in the east and at the glinting sheen of the snow and sighed.

Marco leaned forward against the table. Nick nudged Giuseppe's elbow. "Why, sure!" Giuseppe said. "What dopey guy I am. You want make day's pay on the pick and shovel?"

"Any kind of work," Marco said.

"Okay. I tell Meesta Gardella you one friend come visit me. I fix up." He touched his finger to the stubble on Marco's chin. "But first is better you shave. I see you got the tools. Hurry up. We no have too much time."

While Marco shaved in a little square of mirror tacked against the window frame Giuseppe confided the situation to Tony. Before leaving the house he banged again on the door to Angela's room. "Get up! Get up! Watch you gonna do—sleep all day?" Then the three men started down the road to the village, walking side by side, past the low-vaulted shacks of the colony.

At a distance Luca and Beppo waved their guns and laughed and stuck their fingers to their noses. Giuseppe glanced up at the smiling face at his side, at the firm jaw and the swarthy skin, shining fresh from the razor. "Salamangonia, you good-looking guy when you shave!"

Behind the square rococo architecture of the Gardella dwelling rose the lesser structures of the Gardella enterprises, running parallel to the house with a broad open area between for trucks to maneuver. The huge concrete garage, straight on a line with the driveway which gave out on the main street of the village. To the right of the garage and towering above it, the icehouse, showing a vertical slit on its face, while dumped on the ground before it, tons and tons of ice blocked out of the mill pond waiting to be stored. Further along, huge mounds of sand and gravel with tunnels of big timber through their bowels and the giant conveyer standing apart, like some curious monster stretching its claws to the sky.

At a quarter of eight Federico swallowed the remainder of coffee in his cup, mopped his mustache and folded his napkin. He looked at the vacant chair directly facing him at the kitchen table, at the half grapefruit neatly prepared and setting so dainty with a scoop of mint jelly on top. "Is great life be a doctor," he said. But he hurried to change the subject as he saw a wrinkle gather on his wife's brow. "Good ice we cut this year. Best ice like I never see. Twelve inch. No too thick and no too thin. Just right. I very satisfied with the ice."

"And the olio burner? Or maybe we gotta wait next winter before we have the olio heat?" Giustina said.

"Sangue de la Madonna, you see outside the tank! What you want I do, dig the ditch myself?"

"I spoke to the burner people yesterday," Elena said in a mollifying voice. "If the tank is lowered into the ground today and the trench for the feed pipe dug to the house and the hole cut through the foundation, they can connect up everything tomorrow. That means after tomorrow night we won't have to bother with ashes any more."

"Then everything be nice and clean and we no have dust from the coal no more," Giustina said. "Five years now, I say, is terrible people like us no have olio burner. Is make me real shame when somebody ask, 'Big house like this, why you no have olio burner?' But him, he no want listen to nothing. Who you get for to dig the ditch?"

Federico flung his hand down on the table, palm upward, under his wife's nose. "Please. We no have argumento so early in the morning. For the ice I do what you say. I get fellows from the village what need the work. Okay. Fine. Is

good give work everybody. Is good for my bizaness. Is good
for Emilio. But comes work for the pick and the shovel, is
belong the Italiani up on the hill. The Italiani have the
stomach and must eat too. I no give goddamn what you
say. I no give the work to nobody else."

"He's right. Papa is right," Elena said.

"He right! He alla time right!" Giustina said shrilly. "If
he be right then you eat on the floor like the pig instead
have what you got. But look you bills. Tony! Fifty dollar
from the ice last summer what he never pay. Giuseppe!
Fifteen dollar sand and gravel when he make his foundation. Beppo! Forty dollar from the hondred you lend
him when his house burn up. Bills! Is the money what talk!
Is no feel sorry because somebody is Italiano. We in
America now. If you no have the money you just like dirt.
Is the money send you to college where you no stay. Is the
money make Emilio doctor so he no have to work with his
hands and have car and nice office and meet fine people. Is
the money responsabila for everything."

"But it's hard to force people to pay their bills when they
haven't enough to eat. And if you deny them work——"

A knock came on the back door. Federico rushed to the
window and glanced at an angle out to the stoop. He
turned excitedly to his wife. "Jesu Cristo, shut up! Is
Giuseppe now. You want he hear everything we got to
say?"

Giustina threw down her napkin and walked away into
the living room. Federico stared helplessly at his daughter.

Then he coughed, straightened his body so that his chest and belly described an important curve and walked over to open the door for Giuseppe, who stood timidly holding his cap in his hand.

"I be out in one minuts," Federico started to say. However, his voice dropped as he saw the stranger standing behind Giuseppe on the stoop. He backed off a little and allowed Giuseppe to enter the kitchen. Marco and Tony followed, waiting just inside the door.

"Luca he no feel too good today," Giuseppe said. "So if is all right, I have here somebody else. He need the work and he foist-class on the pick and shovel."

Federico didn't know what to answer. His complexion changed. He looked from Marco to the floor, biting the corner of his lip, pulling the end of his mustache, trying to make up his mind. He turned to Elena for help. She was staring at the man intently. She nodded to her father and smiled.

"You sure he is good?" Federico asked; now he had the approval of his daughter to bolster him.

"Sure I sure," Giuseppe said. "Tell him youself, Marco, how you sling the pick."

"You show me the pick," Marco said.

As the men moved out of the kitchen and Federico went to get his hat and coat he looked at Elena and said in astonishment, "Whyfor you laugh like one silly fool?"

"Just something funny," Elena said. "Just something funny I'm thinking."

Federico brought the picks and shovels from the garage and traced in the snow the size of the excavation. Then he left to go over to his men gathered outside the icehouse. With one of the shovels Marco skimmed away the thin surface of snow covering the frozen earth. Tony lifted a pick and examined the points doubtfully. As Marco stepped aside he swung the pick over his head, grunted and let it come down with all his force. A dull thud; the pick jumped, and nothing to show for the exertion but a tiny hollow in the earth not more than an inch deep.

"Madonna! We be here all year with the picks like this."

"What the hell we care," Giuseppe said as he spat on his hands and stepped beside Tony.

Marco took off his coat and threw it over the tank. He watched Giuseppe's pick come down, and moved into line. Then the blows from three picks began to puncture the stubborn ground, coming closer and closer together until pieces began to chip out and ridges and furrows formed within the oblong area marked by Federico.

At the window of the kitchen, just a few yards away, Elena watched the clots of ice and earth break way and the ground sink under Marco's pick as he cut into Giuseppe's territory. Moving from the window, she looked at the electric clock on the wall and went to the telephone in the hall to ring her brother out of bed and put through another call to the oil burner people.

Around nine-thirty, five inches of the frozen ground had been dug away. The sun warmed and the light snow showed an edge of water. Giuseppe and Tony removed their hunting coats. Federico came over to have a look at the job.

"Is tough like a rock," he said, trying to shift all the blame onto the frost. "No forget here is gotta go one trench for the pipe," indicating against the foundation of the house where the feedline was supposed to enter.

"We no forget," Giuseppe said, marking off the trench.

"Wait," Marco interrupted. "It is only four or five feet. When we finish here it is maybe possible we can dig the trench without touching the ground on top?"

"You think so?"

"If you have a bar and shovel with a long handle?"

"Poogh!" Federico said. "I have everything you want. All kind of equip I got. After when you ready you call. Is good idea—save work like that. Now I go back on the ice." He rocked his head. "Dio mio, so many things I have to watch. One minuts I turn my back and is fifty cents' ice break to hell. And Angelina, Giuseppe? She find some work yet? And the lilla kid, Tony? He is all finish with the cold? You hurry the job, boys. If the tank is no bury today— good-by! Is a storia from my wife I no hear the end."

Marco leaned on the handle of his pick, watching Federico as he waddled back to the icehouse, pompously shouting orders and waving his arms. Through the slit in the front of the building he saw the blocks of ice being arranged in layers and the bulky sections of sawdust-filled doors lifted into place as the layers mounted. Now Federico was directing the men as they set up a slide to haul the ice by means of rope and pulleys and a power winch on one of the trucks. Resuming work, Marco said, "He looks funny, Mister Gardella, but he seems like a nice man."

"Federico all right," Giuseppe said. "I remember when was nobody—just like you and me. Now he big man here. Got plenty money. Own maybe eight house in the village and have mortage on three big farm. You no have to worry for Federico, I betcha."

"Bah!" derisively from Tony. "For what Federico count?" He locked his hands in front of him, indicating Federico's ponderous belly. "He know how to yell and make believe he the boss. He know how to drive that big goddamn car what he got and twist his moostache so he look like rich millionario. Was only one smart thing what he do in his life. Was when his papa send him to Napoli with the vegetable from the farm and he come home with Giustina. Is from there where come the brains. What the hell Federico without Giustina? He chop the ground like a woodchuck—like everybody else from the old country. That's what he do." He paused reflectively. "Is funny one woman with such a face like a mouse have so much brains. . . ."

4

WHEN Emilio had finished his grapefruit and coffee he went out of the house to get his car in the garage. He leaped lightly down the back stoop, hardly noticing the men working at the excavation, and walked over to his father who was standing beside the truck. One of the men waiting for a block of ice at the top of the slide called to him, "Howzit, Doc?"

Emilio smiled. He waved a greeting around. Then he drew his father to one side and confided in a whisper, "I'm going to the hospital now. Probably have lunch with Doctor Stone and go for a couple of drinks somewhere. Better let me have about ten dollars."

"You talk like the money come from the trees," loudly from Federico. "Just before yesterday ten dollars, and now again today. When is gonna finish this bizaness?"

142706

"You don't have to yell," Emilio said. He took his father's arm and urged him further away so the men working on the ice couldn't hear what they were talking about. "In this business it's the connections. Not like your kind of work. You have to cultivate people, maybe spend a few dollars. It's all a part of getting started. If you don't do that you just remain a small-time quack—a nobody, while the fellows who make a splash grab off the dough and become recognized."

Federico's prolonged and stubborn silence caused Emilio considerable annoyance. His lips took on a childlike petulance. "Good God, every time I want a little money I've got to have an argument with you. Do I always have to go to Mamma to get what I want"

"Go ahead. Go you mamma," scornfully. But Federico already had his wallet in his hand counting out the bills. "Here! Ten dollars more. Ten dollars for to make the cultivate. Sangue de la Madonna, you think I was Rockfeller or somebody like that."

Emilio took the money. He jerked up his arm in a quick, mechanical gesture to look at his wrist watch. Then .he glanced down the length of the driveway to the porch of his own dwelling across the street. His eyes fell away from the building and came back along the driveway, settling for a moment on the huge black oil tank and the hunched figures close by.

"Well I'll be damned!"

"Whatsamatter now?"

"That big guy swinging a pick on the end! Where did you get him?"

"Is friend from Giuseppe. Look like a good man, no?"

Emilio slapped his hand against his side. "All the men out of work here in the village and you go and grab a bum off the road. That's smart all right."

"What bum? What you talk? Please, I too busy now for crazy foolishness."

"I mean that fellow there is no more a friend of Giuseppe's than I am. He's just a hobo. Last night he came into the drugstore and tried to steal from the counter. We threw him out and Giuseppe gave him a place to sleep. That's what I mean."

"How I was to know this?"

"By just looking at him. He's got hobo written all over him. You can tell by the way he's dressed. Christ, can't you tell anything about the people you hire?"

There was a pause as Federico stared from his son to Marco in an unbelieving stupor. Then he said with sudden irritation, "Is too late now. He start to work. Elena see him and she say was okay. What you want, I ask to see papers from college to dig ditch?"

"What the hell does Elena know? If you're afraid to fire him, I'll do it for you."

Emilio started toward the tank, but Federico grabbed his arm. "You fire nobody! Goddamn, Jeasuma Christ, every time you come on the job I have trooble. Enough! I no care if the man he just come from prison. You have you ten dollars? Go cultivate what you have to cultivate. Leave my bizaness for me, because now I real mad for fair." His mustache bristled above his sputtering lips.

"All right! All right! Don't get excited. Take it easy. You'll rupture a blood vessel. I was only trying to keep you from making a fool of yourself, that's all."

"Go to hell where you have to go!"

Emilio calmly watched his father pull out a handkerchief and mop his face and mustache. There was no sense crossing him further. He fished into his pockets for the keys to the car and started toward the garage, pausing to look down the driveway again to his office. Suddenly his face grew bright. He waved.

Federico saw the slender girl standing on the steps of Emilio's house holding her coat tight about her hips and smiling. He squinted in an effort to see better. Emilio's car backed out of the garage, made a half circle and came forward through the driveway. He moved aside and then followed slowly in its path, stopping by the oil tank, still staring.

Giuseppe figured something was happening out on the street and stepped out of the excavation to have a look for himself. Tony followed, and Marco. The four of them saw Angela come down from the stoop, walk around the front of the automobile and get inside. Giuseppe turned to Federico. He cocked his head to one side in a proud and knowing way.

Federico managed to force a smile. He waved the men back to work. In a casual manner he crossed behind the tank, tapped it lightly with his knuckles and went up the stairs to the house. Once in the kitchen he grabbed his wife's arm and hurried her into the dining room to the window facing on the street. But it was too late.

Giustina pulled her arm free and looked at Federico as though he had lost his mind.

"Is no me have the whatsamatter," Federico shouted. "You no see what I just see. Angelina—from Giuseppe! She get in the car with Emilio and together they go to the town. Is nothing, that I suppose?"

Elena peered into the room for an instant and cautiously withdrew. Giustina fumbled. She wanted to take the matter lightly and pursed her lips in a manner to indicate as much. But she was troubled.

"And Giuseppe?" Federico stormed. "What you think he think when he see? He look at me with such a big face like to say, 'Ho, ho, Federico, pretty soon we have a nice wedding, no? Make nice match, Angelina and Emilio.' That what he say to me with his face."

"Giuseppe big fool, he think Emilio care five cents for Angelina."

"Is no Giuseppe the fool."

"You just talk from you head," Giustina scoffed. "Is nothing. When Emilio get marry is with differenza stuff from Angelina, I betcha. You see youself the pitch he show me from the girl he go with now. Is high class. Is girl with refine. Is daughter from big man. And you talk from Angelina. You sick upstairs."

"And you too you sick upstairs!"

Federico came close to his wife and tapped the point of his finger against her arm. "Me, I no give one damn if Emilio he marry even a girl from the street. For that I worry? But is no the first time he take Angelina out in the car. I see before and I think nothing. Now is become something else. Giuseppe know. Everybody up on the hill know and make talk. If come something wrong—one lilla slip—good-by all the fancy bizaness for the high-class people and big doctor with American wife and everything else what you have fix so nice for Emilio. Thirty years is no too long time for you forget what is Italiano people when comes one thing like this in the family."

Giustina didn't answer. She sank into Federico's armchair, drawing her narrow shoulders tight into her shawl and staring at the wall opposite like a mute.

"If you no wants something bad happen," Federico said, "is better you talk with Emilio youself. Me, he just laugh. Then I get mad and I break his head with a shovel."

Now Giustina's body rocked back and forth in a monotonous swaying motion. She was working up to an evil mood. Her eyes became tiny luminous coals shining against the dark pallor of her complexion and her scrawny hands pressed deep into the hollow of her lap. Federico backed away, leaving her to herself.

In the living room he went over and stood by his daughter. She was seated at a large mahogany desk going over some accounts on a purchase of sand by the village for use on icy roads. Over her shoulder he watched her check the entries in the ledger against the slips in her hand before making out the bill. In order to change the unpleasant subject of Emilio he said, "You know that fellow outside? He no a friend from Giuseppe. He just a bum."

"So what?"

"So I tell you," Federico answered peevishly. "Santa Maria, I no can open my mouth no more in this house?"

"I mean—who cares what he is so long as he does the work?"

Federico smiled. Under pretext of examining the ledger he bent close to his daughter and affectionately put his arm about her shoulder.

At noon Giuseppe ran over to the grocery store and came back with a loaf of bread, half pound of bologna and two bottles of beer. Tony had brought his own sandwiches. They went over to the garage and sat down on the running board of Federico's big Packard to eat. The men from the village, working on the ice, sauntered off to their houses close by.

Giuseppe removed the wrapping from the loaf of bread. He cut it lengthwise with his knife and then in half. He stuffed in the bologna and handed a portion to Marco along with a bottle of beer.

"I will pay you after," gratefully.

Giuseppe wouldn't listen. He placed his sandwich flat between his palms and pressed it to a reasonable thickness. "I betcha is no the kind bread you like. But today they no have the Italiano. For me, I use by now. Two, three time every week Angelina she buy."

Tony scornfully averted his head and bit through .the thick crust of his own homemade sandwich.

"When you are hungry everything is good," Marco said. He rolled a piece of the spongy dough between his fingers until it became like a ball of putty and snapped it across the garage. "It is what they call air-condition bread. All over you see the signs. It is so full of air and the flour so refined nothing is left." He laughed. "You will not dig many holes with the pick and shovel on this kind of bread."

"Me, I dig my grave before I eat such bread like that," Tony said. "What the hell for I got my wife if I no can have the bread make fresh in the Italiano style with the nice smell in the oven and the fat crust? Is no Tony spend money for the air condition with paper outside and nothing inside and for the pitch what they show to make the people buy. No sir."

Giuseppe had no further comment. Now he was thinking of something else—something particularly pleasant as he swallowed half a bottle of beer in one gulp. He gave a satisfied gasp, wiped his mouth on his sleeve and nudged Tony's shoulder. "You see Angelina how she go to the town with Doctor Emilio? You see that?"

"And what is mean? You know Emilio how he feel for the people up on the hill?"

"Is love," Giuseppe said. "When come the love everything change. Is something inside the man. Nobody can say with who he fall or no fall in love. Doctor Emilio he fall in love with Angelina. What is got to do he like be doctor to rich people? Just the same he Italiano. For him is Italiano girl what attract. No, Marco?"

"Possible."

"Watch you mean, possible? Youself? You like the skinny American girl with no tits and legs like the handle from the pick?"

Marco laughed. "With me, if the face is nice I like every kind of girl. In every shape and every size I find something."

"Just the same," Tony said, "I hope everything is come out all right. I no onderstand this so much free for the girl like I see in this country. No more she have the family to look what she do. Lilla bit school and she tell everybody go to hell and do what she please. Is no joke when the girl swell up and then the man say, what I got to do?—was maybe ten guys fool around before me."

Giuseppe's face went the color of cheese. "Goddamn you!" he yelled, giving Tony a shove which sent him flying from the running board to the ground. "You say something like that for my Angelina and I fix you good!" He stood over Tony, trembling, his fists clenched, one of them clutching the pocketknife.

Marco grabbed Giuseppe's arm. Tony got up. He reached for the sandwich fallen from his hands and brushed the dirt away. "You hothead. That watch you are. I no say anything for Angelina; I just talk for any girl, that's all."

"Shut up you dirty mouth!"

Tony shrugged his shoulders. Marco said, "Tony means nothing bad. He just says it is wise to be careful. He is your friend. Not because he thinks Angelina will do wrong. Because he feels maybe you are pushing too much where it is better go easy and keep your eyes open and save after the headaches."

"Exact what I mean."

Giuseppe finished his beer. Then he walked off by himself and stood leaning against the oil tank with his arms folded. Tony pulled his corncob pipe from his pocket and lit it. He offered some tobacco to Marco, who fashioned a cigarette out of a piece of wrapping paper. They smoked in silence until it was time to go back to work.

Below the frost line the digging became easy. By three o'clock only Giuseppe's head showed above the ground. Federico brought over a crowbar and a long-handled shovel and Marco started to burrow through to the foundation of the house. When the shovel disappeared the full length of its handle and gave a hollow ring Federico called Marco out of the excavation and led him down into the cellar.

"Here," Federico said, handing him a chisel and a heavy hammer. "Where is this mark gotta go a hole about two inch for the feed pipe. You know how to use this tools?"

Marco held the chisel in his left hand and hefted the hammer with the other. He placed the point of the chisel against the mark on the wall and gave it a sharp blow. Before striking again he turned the chisel to cross the indentation.

"I guess you know how to use all right," Federico said. He remained a little while, watching the concrete pulverize beneath the chisel. He watched the man. Several times he seemed to be at the point of asking a few questions but always checked himself, as if what he wanted to say was too delicate for the language at his command.

Out of the corner of his eye Marco saw the short, pudgy legs disappear up the stairs. There was something about Federico made him want to laugh. Something laughable about everyone he'd met so far in this little village: the doctor, Giuseppe, Nick, Angela, Tony. He gripped the chisel and gave an extra smart crack for good measure. An opera came into his head and with it the lilting measures of an aria which seemed to fit his particular mood. He hummed as he worked, his ears sharp for the interludes of silence when he could hear and appreciate his own music.

He didn't see Elena come downstairs. Only when he happened to turn he saw her standing there at his back with her hands in the pockets of her suede jacket and smiling.

He became embarrassed. "I am sorry. I did not know you were listening to my crazy music."

"Don't stop. I like to hear people sing while they work. One of the operas, isn't it?"

Marco leaned over to blow the dust out of the hole now two thirds through the wall. "'Cavalleria Rusticana.' Mascagni. Do you know that one?"

"Not very well," Elena said. "I just recognize the arias, that's about all."

"Shame," Marco said. "You with an Italian mother and father do not know the Italian music. When the opera came to the town where I lived my father always took me. Then when I was in school maybe two or three times every month when I had the money I went. Once in Milano I heard *Traviata* at La Scala. That is something I will never forget. But you—I guess you like better the jazz. What is called the jitterbug, right?"

Elena wrinkled her nose and laughed. Around by the window Federico knocked. He put his hands to his mouth and shouted. "Hurry up with the hole! Is now soon we gotta lift down the tank."

"Okay, okay," Marco yelled back and began to pound the head of the chisel at a furious rate. He winked at Elena. "You see what happens when I talk with a pretty girl. I get into trouble with the boss." Just then a heavy wallop broke the chisel through to the other side and his hand went slamming against the wall. "Madonna!" he hollered, letting go of the hammer and pressing his hand to his chest.

"It's not the boss you have to watch out for," Elena said as he picked up the hammer and chisel again and followed her upstairs to the kitchen. "You sure your hand is all right?"

"Sure. It was nothing—just a little smack. Just a kiss from the wall to remind me next time to keep my eyes on what I do."

But, watching him from the window, Elena laughed to herself as she saw him bend his fingers back and forth and shake his head.

Using short pieces of plank, the oil tank was slowly pried over to the edge of the pit. With the help of Federico the laborers were struggling to shift its position so the holes for the feed pipe faced upward, when Emilio and the druggist came walking along the driveway from the street. They were grinning and talking together in a low, confidential whisper. Emilio seemed particularly elated as he pulled back his right elbow and extended his left arm to the stance for holding a gun, while the druggist's eyes shone large and round with excitement. He had followed Emilio out of the drugstore for a few minutes to see what was going on of particular interest behind the Gardella scene. Now they stood looking down into the excavation, watching the enormous steel cylinder and listening to the grunting exertions. Emilio indicated Marco's back with a slight movement of his head and then pressed his lips together as his father turned around.

"Ho," Federico said, slapping the dust and soot from his

hands, "you back? Is better you go inside right away to see you mamma. She have something to talk to you."

"I know," Emilio said. "Don't worry, I .know what it's all about."

"Everything you know," Federico grumbled, turning his attention again to the oil tank. He looked from the tank to the men as they stood waiting for orders. He scratched his chin.

The druggist walked around the tank. "Christ, what a big bastard! Bet it weighs damn near a ton?"

"One thousand galloni. Is no cardboard."

"How're you going to lower it?"

"Is now what I am try to figure. If no come right, with the holes straight on top, is one salamambitch after to change."

"Get the truck over," Emilio said. "Sling a rope around the middle and lower it slowly with the truck."

Federico considered. He looked questioningly at Marco. "Come on! Come on!" Emilio exclaimed with annoyance. "You'd think it was a Caesarean, all the figuring and hesitation. Hey, Frank! Drive that truck over here! You—with your hands in your pockets! Run over the garage and get a length of rope. Get a move on!"

Both Marco and Tony went running at the same time. Halfway to the garage Tony stopped and waited for Marco as he returned with a coil of rope slung over his shoulder. "Is make me nervous hurry up, hurry up like that," he muttered.

"It is not he makes me nervous. He makes me want to punch him in the nose. I wish the old man sends him in the house or someplace."

Now Giustina stood in the doorway of the kitchen with Elena peering over her shoulder. Giustina called to Emilio. He paid no attention, completely absorbed in the task of showing the druggist, his father, Marco and everyone else the intelligent mechanics of lowering a tank into a pit. He rushed back and forth shouting orders with such assurance and belief in what he was about even Federico was impressed. He stepped alongside the druggist and allowed Emilio full charge.

"Pry her up! Up!" Emilio yelled. "Here. Take the lead out of your pants and sling the rope under. Two half hitches. Wide apart on the bottom and close on top. That's the idea. Christ, it took you a long time to understand."

With the tank cradled in two loops, Emilio attached the end of the rope to the back of the truck, leaving a little slack.

"Come on, you guys. Just push her over the edge of the pit. Then we'll lower her down slowly by backing up the truck."

Giuseppe and Tony hurried to do as they were told. Marco hesitated. "Hey there, spaghet! This is no handout here. Put your shoulders to that tank and shove."

"Sure, boss," Marco grinned. "Only when the tank goes over it will turn and the holes will not be on top any more. They will be on the side."

"No one gives a damn what you think. Get the hell over there and push."

"Wait a minuts. Maybe he right." To avoid argument Federico went over and shifted the loops himself, allowing for the forward roll of the tank as it went over. Emilio waited patiently.

"Ready now? One—two—let her go!"

Federico scrambled out of the way. As he leaped over the mound of earth piled to one side his foot accidently kicked one of the shovels and it went tumbling down into the pit. At the same instant three pairs of shoulders heaved against the tank.

Instead of sliding over the edge as expected, it rolled a half turn, drawing the rope taut, and remained balancing perilously over the mouth of the excavation. Federico held his breath until the tank stopped swaying. Then he stared sheepishly down at the shovel.

"Clumsy! Clumsy!" Giustina called to her husband from the stoop.

Emilio turned to Giuseppe, who was standing nearest him. "Jump down there, Giuseppe, and get that shovel."

Giuseppe looked at the tank and at Emilio. Without a word he slid down through the narrow space left open between the tank and the side of the pit. Marco tried to shout. But it was too late.

The shovel came flying first and then Giuseppe's arms reached up for assistance. There was noticeable relief in the faces watching. Only Marco remained tense as he kept

his eyes on the slender edge of frozen soil which held the
tank from falling. Suddenly the tank jerked and fell forward a few inches. It jerked again. Federico and Tony
struggled to pull Giuseppe out of the pit. As his head and
shoulders appeared the massive cylinder began to slide.

Giustina screamed. Elena averted her eyes. Emilio and the
druggist turned dead white as Marco grabbed up a plank
and made a dive to jam is into the pit beneath the tank.
The tank crashed against the plank, tilted and remained
with one end showing above the mouth of the excavation.

Marco got up. His hands were skinned and full of
splinters. He helped pull Giuseppe out of the pit. Now the
men came running from the icehouse and a crowd gathered
as Giuseppe sat on the ground ready to vomit from fright.

"Here, help him into the house!"

"Wait a minute. Don't move him yet," Emilio said. He
bent down and began to feel Giuseppe's chest and ribs. His
hands were trembling. "How do you feel, Giuseppe? Are
you hurt?"

Giuseppe shook his head, trying to smile. He couldn't
speak.

"Nothing broken," Emilio said. "Don't think there is anything internal. All right, bring him into the house. I'll run
over and get my bag."

Federico sent the men back to the icehouse. Then he
followed Tony and Elena into the house as they supported
Giuseppe between them. As Emilio came back along the
driveway he stopped the druggist and drew a bottle of

whisky from his pocket. He took a drink and handed the bottle to the druggist. Then he saw Marco standing by himself, examining his hands. He went over and offered Marco the bottle. He looked at Marco's hands. "Better come along. I'll give you something to bathe them with."

As they went up the stoop together he said with conviction, "Giuseppe got rattled, that was the trouble. Damn near got himself crushed against the side of the pit. Instead of trying to rush out when he saw the tank coming, all he had to do was drop flat on his belly. The rope would have held. Hold three tanks, that rope. But I guess I was silly to send Giuseppe down. Reflexes too slow. Mind doesn't function in an emergency. Complete mental paralysis. Should have gone down myself, that's what I should have done."

Marco didn't answer. He didn't even smile as he followed Emilio into the house.

AS THE MEN TRUDGED HOME in the dying afternoon, the windows of Wop-Roost threw back dancing reflections of orange and gold. Giuseppe held on to Marco's arm as if afraid he was going to run away. He pointed to the vivid sky in the east and said ecstatically, "See! Tomorrow come another beautiful day like today. We go hunting. I show you what is the real fun what we got here. I show you what is the gun and the good rabbits dog. Huh, Tony, watch you say?"

Tony took the pipe from his mouth. "I say , if was no for the hunt I be rich man like Federico. But when come the frost and the leaves fall down and the dog he no can sit quiet no more, what I care for the money? That what I say."

Marco was silent. For the moment a weariness came into expression and his lips traced a sad, bitter line. Giuseppe pulled his arm. "Whatsamatter? What you thinking? Now for lilla while you stay with me. Jeasuma Christ, is no every day somebody save Giuseppe from be squash like tomato. So no use shake you head and make funny face—I no let you go. Tony here he have one fold cots what he no use. We fix by the stove and you be fine."

"Angelina will not like it," Marco said. "And if I stay I know it will mean trouble."

"Bah!" Tony interrupted. "In my house is me who make the decide for something—no the kids."

"In my house is me too," Giuseppe shouted. "Now enough. Look! I put my hands in my ears. I no want hear no more. You my friend. You save the life from Angelina papa. Shut up now with the talk."

Tony went hurrying off to his own shack where his wife stood waving in the open doorway. She was holding one of the babies in her arms and her black apron bulged out in front, showing another on the way. Tony called, "I be up after to bring the fold cots."

Where the road hesitated before going down over the other side of the hill Giuseppe stopped. He allowed Marco another view of the surrounding countryside, the white farmhouses in the fading light, the land spreading away from the village and far away the houses coming closer together again where the town began. He waited until Marco turned to him and said, "Was no nice thing Doctor

Emilio make me go down for the shovel. If you was happen be someplace else I get maybe kill today."

Marco pretended amusement at the idea of Giuseppe getting himself killed. "Is no that," Giuseppe said. "Is something I no onderstand. You believe maybe is because he a doctor and see so much sickness that he no feel and think no more like other people? Make me wonder lilla bit."

"With that fellow are many reasons why he act the way he does. Is the reason because he is an Italian—poison in his blood. People like you and Tony and Nick, and me even worse, we are just garbage to him. He thinks to be this way makes him different—makes him like the people he tries to copy. But I am afraid. The way I feel inside when that fellow comes near! If I stay too long something will happen sure. Better for you and better for Angelina if I go."

They turned off the road to the house, Giuseppe sucking his tongue, trying to weigh Marco's words and relate them to his own thoughts. Everything merged in a confusion and he couldn't think straight any more. "I guess I getting old now. Everything all mix up. Is hard to tell what is right and what is bad. I try be good papa, but is hard too. For the kids here the life is no more the same like for the old people. Is everything differenza for them. How then I gonna say for Angelina do this or do that when I no onderstand how she feel with my head full Italiano ideas and she have the idea from America and the American school? Is a prooblem never worry me much before. And now is begin to worry me like hell."

He drew a deep breath. ". . . but is no use to talk go away. I make up my head you pay visit with me and, Dio, that I no change for nothing. So no start all over again. But what happen today? I think is better we say nothing inside. For Nick is excuse to get mad and begin shout and curse like crazy bull, and do no good. Maybe too"—Giuseppe scratched his chin and sort of grinned—"maybe Doctor Emilio he so much in love he no think what he do when he send me down for the shovel. Is could be that too, you think?"

"And is possible, too, he is just what they call in English a sonofabitch."

"Just the same is better we say nothing—for now anyways."

That evening Federico ate with his head bent over his plate and slopping up wine one glass after the other, waiting for his son to say something. Emilio was quiet, the sureness and the conceit gone, so that he seemed almost humble with his eyes lowered and his sensitive face drawn serious. At the other end of the table he could feel his mother's glance upon him. The insistency of those little rodent eyes troubled him most because he knew that here was where the real trouble was coming from and it had nothing to do with his father or Giuseppe or money or anything like that. He tried to finish his meal without appearing to hurry. In order to effect an attitude of ease he smiled at Elena several times. But Elena had withdrawn into her own little world. However, it was Elena who started the conversation.

"It's a curious thing about that fellow they call Marco," she said. "He doesn't seem at all like the other Italians we know. He's different in some way I can't explain. This afternoon I heard him singing down in the cellar while he worked. We got to talking and he told me a little bit about himself. I even got the impression he has been to college, because he spoke about going to school when he was grown up and living away from home. But what I mean to say is, he leaves you with a feeling of something positive, that fellow. He's an Italian, and proud of it. Meeting someone like that is a kind of a shock somehow."

"That's it," Emilio said, eager to grasp on a subject to carry him away from the one he was afraid of. "There you have the personification of that stagnant quality which makes the wop looked down upon by everyone else. Refuses to become assimilated, a part of the American way of life. Refuses to mold and shape to the new form of society. These fellows are dangerous, should be eliminated, kicked the hell back where they come from. Jesus, I can't stand those people who talk about the old country and the way things were different and better over there. Why do they come here in the first place?"

Elena drummed her fingers lightly on the edge of the table. Perplexity like a flickering candle shone in the dark orbs of her eyes. She pursed her lips doubtfully. "If it wasn't for that foreigner this afternoon, you might have had something to tickle your conscience right now."

"Bah! It was all dramatics."

"Bah!" Federico repeated with sarcasm. "You get youself a box and make talk on the corner like a politish. Maybe you make more money."

Emilio shrugged his shoulders scornfully and turned to his mother. "Ten dollars I asked him for this morning. I had a date with Stone to arrange for the hunting tomorrow. Good God, a lousy ten dollars when that fellow can do more for me with a few words than ten years' practice in this rotten village. All right, if that's the way it is. The hell with everything. The hell with trying to be a doctor and work up a decent practice. I'll grab a pick and shovel and go and live up on the hill." He threw down his napkin and got up from the table.

Giustina scowled at her husband. She said to Emilio, "Is no the money. The money is for you, Emilio. Is for to help you become big doctor. You ask me when you want." And to Elena, "Keep quiet for what happen this afternoon. Is no we have to worry if the men they get hurt. For what we pay so much insurance every years? Is for that, no?" She took Emilio's hand and made him sit down again. She held his hand, stroking it fondly. "You come you mamma when is something you need."

"Just ten bucks. You'd think it was a fortune."

"Is all right when the money is for you work," Giustina said in a voice exasperatingly sweet.

"And for to take out Angelina and play the big shots!" Federico shouted. He got up from the table and left the room.

There followed a moment of uncomfortable silence for Emilio. He didn't dare look at Elena, who seemed to be thoroughly enjoying his discomfort. He tried to appear amazed and flabbergasted both at the same time.

"Is true you go out with Angelina? You take her for ride many time in the car?" Giustina asked.

"What are you all talking about?"

"Angelina, I talk. Angelina from Giuseppe. You go with her to the town today?"

"So what?" Emilio said, raising his voice indignantly. "She had to go to town to look for a job and I saved her the bus fare. Good Christ, isn't there anything I ever do that's right—that meets with the approval of everybody in this house?"

"Is no the question is right. Angelina Italiana girl from Italiano people. Two, three times you go out and before you know everybody think you serioose and ready for marry. Many things first before you think get marry. And is no the girl for you. Whatsamatter the girl you meet from the dance for the hospital? The one you talk alla time and you show me the pitch in the paper? Is no up on the hill you find somebody like her."

Emilio started to laugh. It began as a low belly gurgle

and increased in volume. He reached over and slung his arm around his mother's shoulders, squeezing her like a little child who has said something terribly funny out of innocence and naïveté.

"Is nothing then with Angelina? You sure?"

"Of course, silly." Emilio continued to laugh. "Imagine me tying up with Angelina. Why, tonight I got a date with Hazel. We're going to a show and then to the Swan Inn. You'll see her someday soon. I'll bring her around. You'll see something all right." He put his fingers to his lips and blew a kiss into the air.

"But just the same you stay away from Angelina. Giuseppe! The people up there! You papa! For something like this I afraid I no be able to help you. Money—anything you want. But, please, no get too close with Angelina."

"That damn wop influence again," Emilio said. "Everything arranged for you—your life, the girl you're to marry and everything else. All right, that settles it. From now on I'll stay clear of Angela like the plague. No sir. No one is going to rope this baby into something. I can promise you that."

Giustina became all happiness again. She hurried to change the subject. ". . . so tonight you have good time? You have the money you need? Fine. And today you see the big doctor at the hospital? You eat with him and you talk? He say you was good doctor too, no? Ha, ha, alla time I say myself is nobody better doctor than Emilio. No matter the money for now. After come all the money you want. First is to meet the people. Maybe he introduce you? He have big party in his house and he invite everybody to meet Doctor Emilio Gardella. He show you where to open office in the town so you have two office—one here and one over there and you be so busy you have two, three nurse to help you with the work. You marry this high-class American girl and——"

"Wait a minute! It's not that easy," Emilio laughed. "But Doctor Stone is interested in me. I'm sure of that. I can tell by the way he talks and asks me questions about my work when I was an interne. If only we can give him a good day of hunting tomorrow! That's all I'm worried about now."

Elena yawned and rose from the table. As Emilio passed her in the hallway to go out of the house he playfully jerked up his fist to watch her spring aside. She stuck out her tongue and screwed her face into a typical expression of Italian distrust. "Everybody think you serioose with Angelina. 'By, 'by you get marry with the shotgun. And I don't mean maybe."

Emilio was due at the Lambertson home at eight-thirty. At eight-forty he was still in the center of town, caught in one of the nightly traffic jams caused by narrow streets of the "horse and buggy days" and a constantly increasing motorized population. He sat at the wheel, beneath the red flare of the signal overhead, cursing the delay and the bloated policeman on his wooden platform for allowing opposing traffic the time of two light changes in an effort to untangle the mess. When the white-gloved hand beckoned he slammed the car into gear so that it almost jumped across the intersection. "Hey there, wise guy!" the policeman shouted. "Go to hell!" Emilio mumbled without bothering to look back.

A little further along he saw a space between two parked cars and swung into it. He got out of the car and hurried along the sidewalk to a cigar store on the corner, working his hand through the fold of his overcoat and into a vest pocket for his address book. He had to wait while a greasy middle-aged woman who looked as if she should have been home washing her husband's socks carried on a conversation about an afternoon at playing bridge.

"Jesus Christ," from Emilio through his teeth. He bought a pack of cigarettes, his own brand, and another with cork tips which he put into his pocket. He tore the cellophane wrapper savagely from his own pack and threw it to the floor.

When the woman finally came out of the booth he scowled at her and stepped inside. He dialed Hazel's number and waited. The maid answered. "This is Doctor Gardella," Emilio said, trying his best to kill the final *a*. "No, don't trouble Miss Lambertson. Just tell her I'll be there shortly. I got caught in a traffic tie-up here in town. Thanks." He hung up the receiver and rushed out of the store.

In about seven minutes he had cleared the central part of the town and was tearing along a wide avenue. Bordering sycamore trees rose gaunt in the lamplight and behind them the vague outlines of fashionable homes at proper distance from each other and separated by ornate stone walls and wrought-iron fences. He swerved the car from the main thoroughfare into a side street, pulling through a semi-circular drive of gravel which struck its arch at the entrance to a large Tudor-type dwelling. He got out of the car, rang the bell and stood waiting. From around in back of the house somewhere a black cocker spaniel came running, yapping its head off and shaking its hindquarters. He reached down and patted the dog's head.

The maid opened the door. Behind her a girl in her early twenties came forward, her hand extended in greeting. She was blonde and tall, with the natural charm and grace of a girl who knows she is good looking but does not allow her beauty to obtrude—relying upon a quiet smile, the soft tone of her voice and her education to accomplish a more enduring effect. "Hello," she said. "I've been waiting. I just spoke to Clara. She's over at the club with Joe Simons and I promised we'd meet them over there. You don't mind?"

"Swell," Emilio answered, holding on to her hand. His eyes traced the sharp silhouette of her body and raised to the lock of golden hair which curled on her forehead from beneath the black turban she wore. "You look marvelous! Wonderful! Am I the lucky guy to be going out with you tonight!"

Through the doorway from the living room a middle-aged woman appeared, clad in comfortable lounging pajamas and smoking a cigarette which she held away from her, tapping the ash into a little bronze tray in her other hand. Her hair, just beginning to silver, showed the ceaseless work of the beauty parlor. She was smiling. "Oh, Mother," Hazel said quickly, "this is Doctor Gardella." Then, turning to Emilio, "Mother always insists on meeting the men I go out with. Old fashioned of her. But that's why she stayed home special tonight instead of going out with Father."

"Just being a mother," Mrs Lambertson said as Emilio appeared a trifle embarrassed. "How do you do, Doctor Gardella. Hazel told me about meeting you at the benefit ball. You must be new on the hospital staff. I don't remember hearing your name before."

"Of course not, Mother. I told you that. He's only been practicing a year. But Doctor Stone thinks he has wonderful possibilities. Didn't you tell me, Emile, you were going hunting tomorrow with Doctor Stone?"

"That's right," Emilio said, finding words at last. "We had lunch together this noon. He was quite taken by the way I handled a case I have at the hospital now. We've planned a little shooting together for the morning."

When they were out in the car Emilio leaned back against the seat with a sigh of relief. "Whew! Your mother certainly gave me the once-over. I didn't know what to say. I hope I didn't sound like a dummy?"

"Nonsense. That's Mother. That's her way. She wants to know about people." Hazel laughed in amusement. "She's a dear. I wouldn't tell you this, but you know it's nonsense so it doesn't matter. Mother was worried when she first heard your name and I told her you were Italian. It was simply marvelous. When she visualizes an Italian all she can think of are those poor creatures who live on Park Street where the charity baskets are delivered on Christmas —or the bootblack, or the barber. She just can't help herself. It's the way she is. That's why you noticed I mentioned the hospital and Doctor Stone. If Doctor Stone likes you, then she simply has to give in."

They were riding along the avenue now, away from the town, the houses spotted further and further apart. Emilio reached for her hand and pressed it lightly to his lips, biting the gloved tip of one of her fingers. "It's amazing. And damnit-the-hell, I know just how your mother feels; that's the funny part of it. But I'll be nice to her little girl. I promise."

"You silly fool," Hazel laughed. She snuggled closer and locked her arm into his. "You're nice, though, you know?"

Their shoulders pressed together. Emilio tried to look at her, at the same time keep his eyes on the road and the headlights of the oncoming cars. "You'll have to kiss me after that."

"And suppose I won't?"

"Well, if you won't, then I'll—I'll take my stiletto and cut your heart out."

"You're such a silly, silly fool," Hazel said and touched her lips to his cheek.

As they approached the low, rambling building of the clubhouse, its lights reaching out into the night, glinting off the polished metal of the automobiles parked in front, Hazel said, "Now if a little later on you can get Doctor Stone to recommend your acceptance into the club, I could have my father second it. It would be grand if you belonged."

"Don't worry, I've been thinking about it plenty. Just let me get a little better acquainted with Stone—that's all. Who is this Joe Simons you were talking about? Must be the son of Simons, the real-estate broker."

"That's right. Just a bore and a snob, but Clara is fond of him. After all, it's her funeral. You be nice to him just the same. No use to get any dislikes on you. We're only supposed to stop for a couple of drinks. But they'll probably want to come along with us dancing. Let them. Clara's a good sport. We'll have fun."

"Okay with me," Emilio said. "If they can put up with him here at the club, who am I to condemn the guy? Listen —with the smell of his father's money I guess he can afford to stick his nose up in the air."

"That's the spirit," Hazel said. "He's just a worm. But even the worms have a place, I suppose."

They entered the clubhouse, passing through the main lounge to the bar. Hazel walked slightly ahead, Emilio following, hat and gloves in his hand, looking to see if he could find the one recognizable face from the hospital. There were a dozen or so people scattered around the lounge, a few in evening clothes, the others in ordinary dress—most of them talking, several couples playing bridge. The women greeted Hazel and looked from her to Emilio. Their eyes appraised him—his dark hair and complexion, his sensitive face, delicate almost to the point of effeminacy, and they found him attractive. The men simply registered a person they had never seen before and wondered.

As they passed into a hallway which led to the bar Hazel turned and stared at a girl sitting in a corner of the lounge by herself. "Just a moment," she said to Emilio, leaving him while she went over to speak to the girl. "Why, Laura!" she said.

The girl smiled wanly. There was something evasive in her manner, strange, a subtle suggestion of fear. It was there in her eyes, in the line of her mouth and the way she spoke when she said to Hazel, "I am so sorry. I've been meaning to call you all week. But I've been so tied up. One thing and another, you know. I'll phone you tomorrow. I promise. We'll get together. . . ."

Hazel joined Emilio again and they started along the hall. Emilio said, "Your friend seems down in the dumps."

"I can't understand. She's so sensitive and peculiar these days. I've hardly seen her. Must be some man, I guess. That's the only thing I can imagine," smiling again.

At the bar Hazel introduced Emilio to a girl with red hair set in reckless curls close to her head. He remembered her from the hospital ball, but her companion he had never seen before. Even in appearance Joe Simons was insipid.

His hair almost white, his eyebrows vanishing to nothing above his pressed-together face reminded Emilio of some kind of a tropical fish. They all had a cocktail together. Joe Simons looked at Emilio and pretended to be puzzled. "Funny," he said. "Gardella? I don't remember my father mentioning that name in the last vote on new members."

Emilio didn't answer. Hazel said quickly, "Don't be funny, Joe. You know Doctor Gardella isn't a member. He's my guest here."

"Aw, I was only kidding," Joe said. "What the hell does it mean to be a member of this morgue anyway? Come on, let's go out where it's lively. Okay, Doc, don't mind me. The place here gives me the creeps." He took Emilio's arm familiarly and led him away from the bar and out through the lounge, with Hazel and Clara following behind talking together in a whisper. Joe was saying, "When I was in college I wanted to be a doctor too. But the governor knocked that idea out of my head. He said the hell go into a profession where you have to build up a practice when you got a sweet business already started for you. That's the old man. Simons Realty Corporation. I'm the junior partner. But I'll bet anything, if I wanted, in six months I could be a first-class surgeon. I've seen you guys work. I know. It's all a knack. Cut open. Chop out what's bad and sew back up again. Simple ABC."

"You got the idea," Emilio laughed. "Like selling a piece of real estate."

"Oh no. There you got something different. You got sales

resistance. You got to figure out your psychology and then pound away with words. Anyway, I say it takes more brains to sell a slice of land than it does to perform an operation."

"Maybe you're right. I'm a doctor; I never tried selling real estate."

When the girls were close Joe said, "Tell you what. We'll race to the Inn. You take the back way. It's a little shorter. I'll go right through town, traffic and all, and I bet I beat you."

"You're insane," Hazel said. "If you think we're going to risk our necks just for your amusement you're crazy."

"Be a sport," Joe said, ignoring her. "Come on, Doc. I'll even give you a head start."

"Let's go!" Emilio cried. As he opened the door of the car for Hazel he pressed her arm. He waited until Joe's flashy roadster zoomed out of the driveway and then stepped on the accelerator to follow. "You're not going to race that idiot, are you?" Hazel said.

Emilio patted her knee. "Of course not. I know his type. Let him beat me to the Inn. Who cares? It'll make him feel good."

Morning again and in the sky little flurries of clouds as stars disappeared and the horizon became clear, sharp. Emilio sat in the kitchen of his house yawning, pulling at the leather thongs of his hunting boots, while the druggist impatiently sipped a cup of black coffee. Emilio laughed. "What a night! I only slept about three hours. Got mixed up with a fellow named Joe Simons. He looks like a fetus. His old man is a big shot at the club and also owns the real-estate firm. And is he a snotty bastard when he gets drunk. There was him and me and Hazel Lambertson and another dame. At the Swan Inn right away he picks a fight with some guy he never saw before. After saving the horse's ass from a shellacking, I had to humor him all night. Now he thinks I am Christ Almighty. Swore he'd have me a member of the club inside a week. And he can do it too. God, what you got to go through to worm your way into that crowd."

The druggist looked at his watch. "If we're going hunting we should have been out of here an hour ago. The deer 'll be through feeding. They'll be up in the hills by the time we get started."

"Just as soon as Doctor Stone gets here," Emilio said. "Take it easy. We got plenty of time. If we don't run across that buck down in the swamp we'll take posts along the run and still-hunt. We'll get a crack at something, don't worry."

"Sure, that's all right for you guys. But I promised the old woman I'd be back by noon to take over the store." Then he added, "You didn't hear Gus Travis tell about the doe he shot the other day? Out after rabbits and the damn thing jumped right in front of him. Had only rabbit shot. Bango, and down it went! Got up again. He followed it for over two hundred yards, pumping rabbit shot into its head before it dropped for good. Bet it looked like a Swiss cheese."

"That's going too far. I can't see that."

"But he got it," the druggist said. "Just the same there's a hundred pounds of nice juicy meat hanging in his attic. Wish it was up in mine—rabbit shot or buckshot or ramming the barrel up its can." He reached into the pocket of his hunting coat and pulled out a handful of shells, sorting them on the table. "How 'll we load?"

"What do you think?"

"I don't give a damn about Wilkins but I ain't taking any chances on a surprise from the game warden. Got the double instead of the repeater. Easier to change shells. Keep loaded for rabbits until we get to the spot. Have two or three slugs handy in a pocket where you can grab them quick——"

"Hold it a second!" Emilio said, rushing through the house to the front door. He hurried down the porch steps to greet the man smiling at him through the window of a new Buick with enamel medical emblems attached to the front and rear bumpers.

"Hello!" he called out cheerfully. They shook hands. "Better pull across the street by the garage over there. We'll use my car. It won't attract so much attention."

"Sure thing," Dr Stone said. "Sorry I'm late. Just my old trouble getting out of bed mornings." He was still smiling. It was a pleasant smile and a part of his personality, just as his ready hand clasp and decisive manner. Dressed in ex-

pensive hunting clothes, with trim mustache and hair spat-
tered gray at the temples, there was a definite note of the
military in his appearance.

Emilio sat down at his side. As Dr Stone drove the car
across the street he said, "Matter of fact I got to bed pretty
late last night. They brought Judge Hartland's daughter in.
A ruptured appendix with peritonitis. Bad. And the family
demands all kinds of attention. I had to stand by all
through the operation. That's one of Stryker's cases. Know
him? A perfect combination of physician, surgeon and
diagnostician if ever I saw one. But his part is mostly the
physician. Never makes a move without consultation and
operates himself only in special cases like this. Smooth? I'll
wager that practice of his is worth twenty thousand a year
if it's worth a cent. You'll have to meet him."

"I'd like to. I've heard a lot about Stryker. Seen him
around at the hospital but never got to know him."

"You will. You will. Only last night we were talking
about you and that case you have with us now," Dr Stone
said. He had a habit of making his words ring out and pausing between sentences to clear his throat, so that what he
had to say took on added importance. He swung the car off
to the side of the garage and parked it.

As he stood with his gun slung carelessly under his arm,
waiting for Emilio's coupé to back out, his interest was
caught up by the icehouse, the mountains of sand and
gravel and the monstrous architecture of the residence.
Nothing seemed to escape his attention. When the car

stopped he was standing in the center of the driveway appraising Emilio's simple white dwelling across the street. Instead of getting inside, he jumped on the running board for the short distance.

"This is the right way," he said when they were on the porch. "A man should be on his own from the start. You live here by yourself, don't you?"

Emilio nodded. "My family lives over there. Once in a while my mother or my sister may come over to straighten things a bit. Otherwise I'm by my lonesome. It's the only way. I've got privacy and no one to go nosing into my affairs —that is, when I have any affairs." He laughed in a manner which the older man seemed to understand and appreciate.

The druggist was pacing the floor in the waiting room, anxious to get started. "Wait a minute," Emilio said, "we'll have a snort first. How about it, Doctor Stone—a little something under the belt to brace us against the cold?"

"Splendid idea."

"For Christ sake, bring the bottle along," the druggist grumbled.

"Sure we'll bring the bottle along. But for luck we've got to knock one off now." Emilio disappeared into the consultation room for a minute. He left the door open and Dr Stone peered inside. He nodded approvingly at the gleaming cabinets and the meticulous arrangement of instruments, at the chromium fixture overhead and the adjustable lights on the side of the examination table. Emilio handed him a tumbler of whisky. He swallowed it in a

quick gulp and walked over to a taboret on which an oblong case rested. He looked inside. "An electrocardiograph
recorder! Why, man, you're right up to the minute here!"

"Down to the last scalpel approved by the medical society," Emilio said proudly. "Everything new. I even had
the place redecorated before I moved in." He urged along
into the hallway and showed his sleeping quarters which
with the modern studio bed also served as a rest room.

"You must have other rooms upstairs?"

"Two more bedrooms and another bath. Never use them,
though, except when I have some of my old school chums
up from the city."

The druggist stuck his head into the hall. "If we don't
get a move on we might just as well stay the hell home."

"Good God," Dr Stone exclaimed, looking at his wrist
watch, "five past seven! Come on. Come on. We'll never
get started at this rate. Professional stuff be damned today.
Where did I leave my gun? Everybody ready? Show me
that buck you were bragging about, Gardella. Just one peep
at him over the top of the barrels. That's all I ask and I'll
gladly set my gun away till next year. But this way, without
even a shot all season? The devil! Onward, lads. The smell
of powder and the stricken game. How far do we have to
go?"

"Just a few minutes' ride over the hill."

The three of them squeezed into the front seat of
Emilio's coupé. Dr Stone sat in the middle and the druggist
sat on the outside with the guns between his legs. As the

car sped past the low commercial buildings and turned up the hill leading to Wop-Roost and the open country on the other side, Dr Stone said, "There's no danger? The game warden, I mean. It would be rather annoying, and embarrassing—for me anyway."

"Danger hell," the druggist said. "Just let me see a pair of horns sticking up through the brush."

"You don't have to worry," Emilio assured. "In this territory we assume all responsibility. We take care of everything. All you know you're out hunting rabbits, that's all."

6

THE HUNTERS of Wop-Roost had gathered outside Giuseppe's shack to talk over plans for the day. There was Luca with his spaghetti belly buckling and unbuckling his belt. Vincenzo, lean and hungry looking, like a pair of stilts with boots on. Beppo wiping his nose on the frayed cuff of his hunting coat with the dark bloodstains all over it. Tony sucking the end of his corncob and grinning the grin of a chimpanzee. Giuseppe, small, delicate in build and with the worry always on his face. Marco, tall, healthy and smiling, dressed in clothes loaned him by Nick and testing the balance of an old single-barrel shotgun by jerking it to his shoulder. And the hounds! The lop-eared little mutts jumping about excitedly, running off, coming back again, fighting among themselves.

"Is hope we have good luck today," Luca said. "Salamambitch, one lousy rabbits yesterday. Is no enough for my lilla Gioacchino."

"Today we lucky sure," Tony said. "Everything right. Is no wind. Is no too cold. The rabbits they be out sure today."

"Poogh! Listen the professor," Beppo said. "Is all teoria. You know what is the rabbits think for the teoria? With the tail they tell you. When is feel like come out they come out. When no feel like, go to hell teoria and everything else. But you know how is gonna finish this monkey bizaness hunt all day and no game?"

"How is gonna finish?"

"Is gonna finish"—Beppo glanced from side to side to make sure no woman was around—"is gonna finish I gonna have plenty meat."

"You sick in the head," from Giuseppe. "Is here the policeman he watch. Is here the game warden have his eyes alla time. Gonna finish you make plenty trooble for everybody."

"Sure," came from Luca. "Everybody watch here. When is something for to blame is the wop-guinea first every time. But you see for youself pass the car from Emilio. You see Meesta George from the drugstore. I betcha you think is for the rabbits they go? I betcha you got the wood for the brains."

"Va-va! Is better we talk no more for this thing," Giuseppe said. "How we gonna hunt? I take Tony and Marco and we hunt by Smith Farm and the swamp. You go with

Beppo and Vincenzo down other side by the lake. For lunch we come back. If we no have luck we try someplace else."

As the two groups were about to separate Nick leaned out of the window and yelled to Giuseppe, "Where you hunt? You hunt by Smith Farm?"

Giuseppe nodded and Nick hollered to Marco, "Is the place what I tell you last night. Look yourself. See if you can find one dirty shame thing like that except in America." He rested his arms on the window sill and watched the hunters disappear through the thick blackberry cover, on their way down the other side of Wop-Roost.

Now the tangle growth of the hillside merged with the fields and orchards of an abandoned farm. The entire countryside spread before Marco's eyes in an undulating sea of dry goldenrod and unmowed timothy, while the house and barn in the distance appeared like imaginary arks floating along. To the left, nestling between gentle rounded hills, stretched a wild expanse of marsh.

The dogs ran on ahead, only the flagging of their white tails visible above the weeds. Giuseppe led the way over a stone wall into an orchard. He waved his arm around. "Is here call the Smith Farm. What Nick he tell you?"

Marco paused under an apple tree. He kicked at the frozen fruit lying on the ground, turned the color of cow dung, nibbled by the rabbits and crushed by the passing feet of hunters. His gaze followed across the orchard to a vineyard and came to rest on the farmhouse, drab, sullen in appearance because of lack of paint and repair. He shook his head. Giuseppe said, "Is belong to Federico. He get for the mortgage."

"I know. Nick told me the story. But why? Why?"

"You ask me?"

"Is it because the farms around here do not pay any more? Fake! The land always pays. The land will always support the man who works it. Up on the hill you have Nick; you have many poor people who know the ground and who know how to make it produce. Why does not Federico Gardella rent this farm to them and let them pay from the crops?"

"You tell that to Giustina."

"I will tell you why. It always comes back to the same story. In Italy you were a farmer? Poogh, for the farm and the wop who stinks from the ground and never gets rich! You are in America here! The factory and the machine and the business. Make the money. Nobody cares that you were a good hand to do this and to do that. The money what counts. I am ten thousand dollars better than you. I got the kids in college. Julio, to be lawyer. Antonio, a dentist. Maria, a schoolteacher. Why the hell do I want to remember what I was? I am an American now. My name is no more Angelo Pastrami and maybe my kid will be president someday."

Up ahead one of the hounds let out a piercing wail. Tony called, "Hey! We gonna hunt or we gonna talk?"

"Come on," Giuseppe said, grabbing his gun under his arm and hurrying down between the rows of apple trees.

He jumped on a stone wall and motioned Marco down to the other end as Tony cut diagonally across the orchard to take a post on the other side.

The dogs hunted in the middle, one behind the other, with noses low to the ground and stopping now and then to raise their throats in a weird lament. Marco waited with his gun ready, balancing on the field-stone fence. Gone was the anger and the surging resentment of a moment past. It was the hunt now, the breathless thrill of dogs baying and eye sharp for the quick movement of game. Here was something real for a man, something in the bones and in the blood which swept away, 'way back into the past. He saw a quiver through the grass and felt the quivering response in his own body as he brought the butt of the gun hard against his shoulder and pressed the trigger.

Giuseppe and Tony came running. "You get him? You shoot?" Marco picked up the dead rabbit and held it by the ears, allowing the dogs to sniff, patting each one on the head as a reward.

"Ah, is a nice rabbits!" Tony said, running his fingers through the light fur of the belly. "Salamangonia, I see poof, poof in the grass but I no have time to shoot."

"Was good shot," Giuseppe said. "Is no easy shoot rabbits in high stuff like this."

"You bet your life it was a good shot," Marco said as he slipped the rabbit proudly into the game pocket of Giuseppe's coat. He took off his cap and wiped his arm across his brow. "Even my father would have said it was a good shot. And from where I come there was only the mayor better than him."

"You hunt on the other side?" Tony asked in surprise.

"Sure he hunt. Watch you think? Is no for the clothes you can see is a gentlaman we got here. You betchamylife his papa have big property over there and private place for to hunt and Marco he know the gun from a lilla kid, just like the son from real gentlaman. Huh, Marco—I am right?"

Marco smiled indifferently. He threw the gun over his shoulder, holding it by the barrel. "There is no use to talk about the past now." However, Tony was still looking at him, deeply perplexed.

Marco nudged him good-naturedly. "Come on, Tony. We have many rabbits to shoot yet. Today we hunt and have a good time. Tomorrow we worry about the problems." He began to sing an old Italian mountain song.

Tony's face beamed. He reached into the pocket of his hunting coat and pulled out a flat bottle and passed it around. "Go to hell the trooble! Everybody have trooble. Only the hunt make you forget. The nice dog what you have train youself. The friends. The wine. Then you no worry too much. Is this keep the poor bastich Italiano alive."

They covered the orchard and then the vineyard where the grapes had shriveled on the vines, furnishing food for the pheasants and the grouse and the winter birds. The dogs started up another rabbit, but it headed straight for a field-stone wall and vanished into intricate passageways and tunnels. They tried the open fields and tangles of thorny brush where the dogs couldn't enter, beating with their guns in an effort to drive the rabbits out.

"Where now?" Marco asked.

"Down the swamp," Tony said. "Big goddamn swamp rabbits there like you never saw."

Giuseppe pointed to the black outline of an automobile parked off the side of the road where it dipped down past the swamp. "Is no such a good idea. Doctor Emilio and Meesta George hunt over there."

"What we care? Is no posted land. Is for anybody to hunt."

"Sure. But is no for to hunt without licenza."

"Ah, Marco! I no remember that."

"Do not worry about me," Marco said. "If the hunting is good over there, we will go. In a big swamp like that there is very little chance to meet anybody. Then I just drop the gun."

"I suppose is the drugstore gonna talk?" Tony scoffed. "A bastich like him he shoot his mother if he think she is good to eat."

"Is better we hunt someplace else."

"Aw, shut up! Alla time is something with you." Tony took hold of Marco's arm and started to march off ahead. Giuseppe lagged in the rear. At the edge of the swamp Tony held the dogs and waited for Giuseppe to catch up. "We work it like this," he said. "I take the middle with the

dogs. Giuseppe, you take the side over there, and Marco the
side under the hill. We go easy and let the dogs work.
If is a rabbits in there, somebody gonna get a shot. Okay?"
  "Okay."
  Tony waited until both Marco and Giuseppe had taken
their positions. He waved his gun and then started through,
speaking encouragement to the dogs, whistling softly so as
to prevent them from hunting too far in advance. For
some fifteen or twenty minutes they hunted through the
marsh in this fashion.
  Marco followed the fringe of the swamp to the right of
Tony. On either side low wooded hills stretched away into
the north like charging buffalo. He strolled along between
clusters of white birch trees, swinging his gun, waiting a
warning from the dogs. Now and again he could see one of
them leap over a frozen mound of swamp grass. Sometimes
he caught sight of Tony laboriously making his way
through the difficult brush growth, and Giuseppe far away.
But for the most part it was as if he were alone in the
midst of this winter desolateness and the snapping of twigs
and branches underfoot gave accent to the feeling.
  He came out of the birches to a clearing where the dry
grass bent low and red against the earth. He was about to
cross when suddenly he was startled by a rapid series of
shots fired close by..The shots came from his right, up the
hill. Backing away quickly, he dropped the gun and covered it over with dead leaves. Before he could jump to his
feet again he heard a crashing through the thicket as a big

buck deer staggered blindly across the clearing and plunged into the swamp some distance ahead. Then he heard voices, and in another moment the dumpy figure of the druggist came into view, followed by Emilio and the man he had never seen before. He stared at the three hunters.

When the druggist caught sight of Marco he got scared and stopped dead. Dr Stone stood to one side, awkward, embarrassed, the gun clumsy in his hands. They were both a little pale as Emilio swaggered up to Marco.

"Come on! Don't stand there like a goddamn fool. Which way did he go?"

"Who?"

"You know what I mean."

Marco didn't answer. Now Tony came running out of the swamp, followed by the dogs and Giuseppe close behind. "Whatsamatter?" Giuseppe asked in a quaking voice. "This hobo sonofabitch——" Emilio started to say. Then he saw the dogs. "Hey, Tony! Get those dogs over here!"

"Wait!" Marco shouted. "Hold the dogs, Tony. Do not let them loose. First we will teach this fellow how to talk when he wants something." He whirled quickly and yanked the gun from Emilio's grasp and threw it to the ground. "Now what did you say before? What did you call me?"

The druggist and Dr Stone ran and grabbed hold of Emilio. He tried to break away. "Let me go! Let me go! I'll break every bone in the bastard's head!"

"You will break nothing," Marco said calmly. "You are just wind. A big bluff. That is what you are."

Dr Stone bent close to Emilio. He whispered sharply, "Let's get out of here, Gardella. This is no mix-up for us. We can't afford any unpleasantness."

There were tears of rage and humiliation in Emilio's eyes. He picked up his gun and allowed himself to be led away across the swamp. But before he was out of sight he turned around and cried in a voice broken and shrill. "You sonofa-bitch! You'll be sorry you were ever born before I'm through with you."

"Go to hell!" Marco yelled back.

All the way back to the village Emilio was silent. He sat with his hands gripped tight to the steering wheel and staring at the road as it disappeared beneath the car. Dr Stone said, "If they don't talk, I wouldn't worry too much if I were you. Maybe he didn't see the deer. It's possible he didn't. Far as I'm concerned, I'm satisfied. I got my shot at a buck this year. That's what I was interested in."

"Hell, he didn't see it," the druggist said. "You saw how he was afraid to let the dogs loose. They'd-a picked up the trail in a second. And those other two! Not the big guy. They're his patients. Can you imagine that?"

"An appreciative lot, I must say."

Over the crest of the hill the shacks of the little Italian colony came into sight. The druggist pointed. "Here's where they live. Wop-Roost, that's what we call it down below. A good name too. In the winter you can see the tar-covered shacks over there and they look like vultures roosting."

When they reached Emilio's house the druggist ran off to relieve his wife at the store. Dr Stone stopped for a few minutes. Emilio mixed a highball. As they clicked glasses he said, "Here's to the deer we didn't get." His face was serious.

"Don't take it so hard, man! It's all in the game. They probably need the meat more than we do. Anyway, you didn't kowtow to the beggars. Beneficium accipere liberatum est vendere. The next time they need you let them howl. Though a lot that practice can mean."

"I'll fix him," Emilio said stubbornly.

There followed a silence. Dr Stone looked into his highball glass, at a little square of ice floating in the sparkling gold liquid. Then his eyes wandered across the room, through the open door leading into the consultation chamber and back to Emilio again. "This office you have, Gardella. All the expensive equipment. Mean to tell me you can keep going with the sort of practice you've got?"

"What? I'm sorry—I didn't——" Emilio stammered.

"I mean—those Italians, and maybe a few other poor patients! I don't see how you can make it pay."

"Oh," Emilio said. "You're right. That is, I don't make any money to speak of at the present time. But I am working along. At least I try to give all the benefits of a modern doctor's office I can afford. And I don't figure on things always remaining the way they are. There's the hospital. My recognition there . . ."

"Yes. Yes, of course," Dr Stone said. He swallowed the contents of his glass and got up. "Well, I'd better be getting back now. Why don't you give me a ring at the hospital Monday? I'll see if maybe we can't have lunch together or go out for a few drinks. On me this time?"

They shook hands. Emilio mumbled a few more excuses about the deer, but Dr Stone wouldn't listen. However, Emilio followed across the street to the garage and waited as Dr Stone got into his car and backed it around. They shook hands again through the window and the big Buick went speeding off through the noonday light.

Over in the firehouse at the other end of the village a deafening blast from the siren announced the cessation of labor for the week. Emilio didn't move. The men working in the icehouse passed and he greeted them mechanically. His mother called to him and he started to walk slowly toward the house, stopping at the excavation. He saw the copper tubing which had just been fitted to the tank, the filling pipe extending up to a level with the surface of the ground and the bronze screw cap. He noticed everything, and yet registered nothing. His mother called to him again. His father came over from the icehouse and stared at him in astonishment. "Whatsamatter, you sleep?"

"Oh," Emilio said with a start. "It's you!"

"No, your grandmother."

Giustina appeared on the stoop. When Emilio came near she took his hand and drew him into the house. She could hardly talk for her excitement. "Why you keep me waiting? All morning I sit by the window. When I see the beautiful car with the sign from the hospital I get so excite I no can do my work. What happen? You have some luck? Doctor Stone, he have a good time? He ask for you to visit him? Dio mio, whyfor you no talk?"

Elena and Federico were listening. Emilio straightened. "Don't worry about me and Doctor Stone. We're getting along fine." Then his expression changed and he turned suddenly to his father. "Those lousy bastards you've been giving work to up on the hill!"

"Wha—wha——"

"Wha—wha—— I'll tell you what. I'm going to get that goddamn hobo run out of here if it's the last thing I do. Why? I'll tell you why! We shot a buck and it ran down into the swamp right in front of that skunk and he wouldn't tell us where it went. And not only that. He got snotty. He wouldn't let Tony lend us the dogs. By Jesus, I'll show him."

Giustina clasped her hands together and began to rock her head. Federico yelled, "What you gonna do? Is maybe five-hundred-dollar fine for shoot a deer and you gonna make stink. Is one crook gonna bring the police for the other crook. Dio, santa miseria, bestia! This bizaness for to be doctor gonna make me kill somebody yet! What you can do? What you gonna do, stupid jackass fool!"

"I'll show you. If you think I'm going to let a dirty green-horn put it over on me you've got another think coming." He rushed over to the telephone in the hall and dialed a number.

"Hello! Hello! Mrs Wilkins? Doctor Gardella calling. The sergeant home? No? Back late in the afternoon? All right. Tell him to stop by my office. Doesn't matter. Later the better. Thanks." He slammed down the receiver. "We'll see what I can do."

"The crook and the more crook police. Bah, I wash my hands from everything!" Federico went close to his son, trembling, shaking his finger. "Su mia madre! I swear. If is a fine to pay, you rot in the prison before comes one penny from this house. Is no use you mamma. Is no use nobody. No one penny. Remember!" With that he went storming out of the house to sit in the sanctuary of his big Packard.

"If Doctor Stone no mad, is better forget about the deer," Giustina said to Emilio. She was angry too but, at the same time, a little afraid. "For Giuseppe and Tony don't worry. I know how is the best way for to fix. Elena! Put you coat. Make the bills. Now we see if they be so smart like they think."

"The hell I'll forget about the deer," Emilio said.

"What do you think you can do?" Elena asked quietly.

"Not a damn thing. But I'll have Wilkins throw a scare into those wops they'll never forget. When he gets through with them we'll see where that wise guy stands. They'll throw him out on his ear so fast he won't know whether he's coming or going."

"Enough with the talk," Giustina said. "Is only one thing with the people like that. Is the money. Hurry up, Elena! Make the bills."

7

NICK sat at the table watching Giuseppe run the point of his pocket knife into the skih of the rabbit and start to clean it. He had been sitting quietly for some time. Something was wrong. He could tell by Giuseppe's silence and the look on Marco's face. Finally he said, "Is must be very good the hunt this morning, everybody feel so good."

Giuseppe looked up from the rabbit and glowered. He lowered his eyes again as Angela came in from the kitchen. She was wearing a new printed-silk dress with an apron tied around her middle. Her hair was freshly curled and her complexion vivid from recent scrubbing and make-up. Even the lipstick had been carefully applied, though she knew it would have to be put on again before she went out.

"If you were hunting down back," she said, "you must

have come across Emile and Doctor Stone from town? I saw them pass a little while ago." She smiled secretively. "This was a big day for Emile. He's been planning it for a long time."

Giuseppe didn't say anything.

"Ho, ho!" from Nick.

"Why, what's the matter?" Angela said, her eyes nervously on Marco.

"Is nothing," Giuseppe said. "You have eat for you? All right. Then you go where you have to go."

Marco got up. "If she is to hear the story, it is better she hears it up here first." He said softly to Angela, "I had a fight with Doctor Emilio. He called me names I do not like and I got mad and told him to go to hell."

"You! You had a fight with Emile?"

"Yes," Marco said. "And I will tell him again if it is necessary. I am sorry, for you. But for everybody else up here I am glad."

"Good!" Nick cried. "And if you have poonch his face I tell you thank-you myself."

Giuseppe tried to explain. He took Angela's arm and said, "Is no for to get all excite. Was something for the hunt. He talk bad to Marco and Marco talk back."

"I don't care what it was," Angela said, tearing away from her father and standing in front of Marco, her small white fists clenched and her face tight with anger. "Isn't it bad enough the way things are, without you coming here to make more trouble? Why don't you go where you belong instead of staying here and eating our food and making it harder for us? Go on back on the road!"

"Shut up!" Giuseppe said. "Marco he pay me for everything he eat. Is more than what you know he do for me. Now keep quiet for the talk like that or I let you have one slap make you head ring. Onderstand?"

"I won't shut up!" Angela cried. She tore off her apron and flung it to the floor. "I know what he is. Emile told me all about him stealing at the drugstore. He's just a tramp and a thief who thinks he's somebody."

Quickly and deftly Giuseppe's hand shot up. The flat of his palm against Angela's cheek made a sharp sound. She gasped. The words in her mouth nearly choked her. Giuseppe followed her with his hand raised as she backed away into her room. He closed the door and then sank weakly into a chair. "I tell you was do no good say anything to her." He sat with his hands folded between his knees and his head lowered as Marco told Nick what had happened.

While they were eating, Tony entered followed by Luca, Beppo and Vincenzo. Luca stretched out on Nick's couch and unbuckled his belt to make room for the spaghetti swelling his paunch. Beppo sat on the cot while Tony and Vincenzo sprawled comfortably on the floor. Giuseppe handed the wine gallon around. "Is everybody now I guess know the storia," he said.

There were silent nods.

"Salamangonia, I betcha was my deer," Beppo said.

"Sure, was the rabbits Emilio and the drugstore go to hunt," Luca said.

"Is no time for the joke," Giuseppe said. "Is very bad bizaness. The deer he dead in the swamp. Doctor Emilio he mad like hell. And Meesta George he mad. And is a big doctor from the town."

"Is smell something I no like," Vincenzo said.

"Smell trooble," from Luca.

"Smell the game warden," Beppo added.

"Whyfor he no tell them where the deer go?" Vincenzo said, pointing at Marco. "Was they deer. Whyfor we have to be mix up? The Italiano no can fight with the people down below. Everybody up here know that. But him he think different. Is him now to worry what he gonna do."

Nick turned to Marco. "Bah! Listen the lilla chicken. Cluck! Cluck! Go under the wing you mamma and you be safe. And when you walk on the street even the birds they crap on you head."

Vincenzo turned red. "Sure," he shouted, "what the hell you care? You have nothing. You no give goddamn. Comes the trooble, tomorrow you move someplace else. You. Him. But we, we gotta stay here. And if Emilio no say nothing? And if Meesta George keep his face shut? Somebody else find. And who you think get the blame?"

Marco now stepped to the center of the floor. He stared at the faces all around him and pityingly at Vincenzo. "Nobody will get the blame because I will go myself to tell the game warden what has happened."

Astonishment, stark in all eyes. Lips sputtered but nothing came forth. "And he will believe me," Marco said, "because I will show him the deer and I will tell him who killed it and tell him the names. You want me to do that?"

"Wait a minuts," Giuseppe said. "This is no necessary."

"But for me it is necessary," Marco said in a firm voice. "If the law is broken and somebody is to be blamed, it is the people who break the law. The man from the drugstore. The doctor from the town and Doctor Emilio. Angelina says I am a crook. Doctor Emilio told her that. But now is the time to see just how everything stands."

Giuseppe started to excuse Angela. Marco motioned with his finger to his lips. He held his eyes on the door of Angela's room. Slowly it opened and Angela came out. She was dressed to go to the village and had been waiting, listening behind the closed door. Now her anger had given way to another expression. Marco pretended not to notice. He reached to the nail on the wall for his hat and coat.

"Come on," Nick said. "Angelina no mean nothing. She no wants you make trooble for Doctor Emilio."

"I am sorry. I am going away from here now," Marco said. "But first I want to be sure the right people get blamed for the trouble you say I am making for you."

As Marco placed his hand on the doorknob Angela covered her mouth and uttered a low cry. He turned and she lowered her eyes to the floor. Nick hopped up and forced him to take off his hat and coat again. "You see! She was only make fool with you." He waved Angela out. "Go on,

Angelina! You go the village and have good time. We keep Marco here. We make sure he no say nothing."

Marco watched Angela through the window until she had disappeared down the road. He laughed and picked up the gallon from the floor, allowing the wine to trickle down his throat with a gurgle. "Now I have listened enough to all this foolishness about the deer. It makes me vomit this talk about be afraid do this and be afraid do that. You hear!" He slammed his fist down on the table so that the plates jumped.

"What you want we do?" Giuseppe asked.

"Or we tell the game warden, or we get the deer. I say the meat is for the people who need it. And that is not Gardella, or the man from the drugstore or the big doctor. That is what I say."

"He right," Beppo argued. "Is nobody need the meat like us. We hunt and we hunt and never break the law and when comes something every salamambitch point his finger up here. This time be different for change. I go with Marco myself to get the deer."

"And I go too," Luca said.

"Bravo!" Nick shouted. "Was no for the leg I carry him home by myself. We see if the poor Italiano no can play the bastich just like the rich people down the hill."

Vincenzo shook his head. He was scared. Giuseppe was a little scared too and so was Tony. Vincenzo said, "And this is exact what Emilio figure. Then you see how you be so smart! If Giuseppe want the deer here, all right. Me, I stay my house. I no have nothing to do with this kind dirty work."

The argument went on. Suddenly Giuseppe sprang up and pointed through the window. "Ah, is come the first visit already. Look!"

They all gathered to watch Elena as she stopped along the road to wave and talk to the women in the shacks further down. In characteristic fashion she sauntered up the hill, her body a little slouched, her hands deep in the pockets of her fur coat and her beret pushed back on her head so that her black hair curled around it. She was smiling, apparently at ease with these people whom her brother found so distasteful.

Giuseppe rushed to clear the dishes from the table. When Elena entered she was greeted in Nick's cheerful, "Allo! Allo!" Marco offered her a chair. The others just smiled sort of sheepishly and stood around embarrassed as Giuseppe poured a gentle portion of wine into a clean glass. Elena held the glass in her hand. She said to Marco, "I met Angela on the way up. She gave me to understand you promised not to make any trouble for Emilio. Thanks. I'm sure he'll appreciate that."

"Who make troouble?" Giuseppe said. "Was just talk for Angelina. Was nothing."

"Even if you wanted to you couldn't. You think your word would mean anything against Emilio or the druggist or Doctor Stone?" She talked straight at Marco, ignoring the jumble of comments and excuses from all sides.

"If you get the game warden, I take the risk of six months in prison to prove he will believe what I tell him."

"You have confidence anyway."

"I have not been in this country long enough yet to lose that. And it is not your brother or the druggist or the other one strong enough to stand in front of the law and say it was me who killed the deer. Any time you want to make the proof I am ready."

Elena sipped the wine in her glass. "But why didn't you tell them where the deer went?"

"For the same reason," Marco said. "Nobody calls me a goddamn fool and I hurry to do what they say. When you see that I hope you see me choke first."

"And the deer is dead?"

"Like a rock," Tony said.

Elena took an envelope out of her pocket. She stared at it pensively, folded it in half and pushed it into her pocket again. She finished her wine. "I'm taking a walk up the road a ways," she said to Marco. "Maybe you'll show me the deer? I'd like to see it."

"Is way in the swamp," Giuseppe said. "You get you clothes all scratch."

"That's all right. The shoes are old and the stockings don't matter."

Tony was about to suggest going along too but he caught Nick's eye. Marco put on his coat. He didn't bother to take his cap. He opened the door to allow Elena to pass and then followed. As the door closed Nick clasped his hands together and shook them at the ceiling with a laugh.

Elena and Marco walked leisurely along the road leading down the other side of Wop-Roost. The silence between them grew uncomfortable. When Marco looked at her questioningly Elena said, "I only wanted to tell you something I couldn't tell you inside. Wilkins—that's the policeman around here—you'll see him tonight. And if he finds the deer in the house it'll be just too bad. Try and convince him then."

"You are sure?" Marco asked.

"Sure of what?"

"Sure the policeman will come?"

"Course."

"Then you can be sure he will find the deer."

"All right. Be obstinate. I was only trying to help you. If you get the Italians into trouble it'll be your own hard luck. You might just as well pack up and start moving again."

"Oh no. I do not think I will move so quick," Marco laughed. "Every day I find something more here I like. Maybe I will stay. Maybe the traveling is over now—who knows? But if I stay it is to be like that big tree you see over there. Feet on the ground and head up in the air, and not the little wind will blow me down every time. And it is not to live in a shack on the top of the hill and be like the people down below want me to be. No. Too much I have left behind just to find that."

"But I can't understand. You're an Italian and you'll

never be anything else. America is no place for you. You ought to go back."

Marco was a long time answering. He picked a pebble from the road and juggled it in his palm. "Sometimes when I am discouraged I think like that myself. But that is wrong. There is no more a place for me over there, or the men like me. It is here I belong. Here the country needs people who can bring to it something. Not the people who just come to take the money and the easy life. Not the people who hurry up to get rich because they believe it is this what makes them American. It is here I will stay and stay like I am—Italian. And I will grow. And out of the love for the good in what I remember from over there and the love for the good in what I find here, there will come—there will come——" He struggled with the phrase, trying to shape it with his hand. Then he smiled. "Anyway, what will come is not some jackass to work on the machine when he should be out in the field planting potatoes. . . ."

Now the road curved down through the valley. On one side the marshland and on the other the abandoned farm where the valley began and the brook cutting through from the hills, laden with ice and bright in the sun. They stopped. Marco turned his back to the farm and pointed far into the swamp. "It is a long way if you want to go in."

"I don't think so," Elena said. "I love to see the deer alive and running in the woods. And when they stand still—suddenly erect, with their nostrils spread and their eyes wild. But a dead deer? I never liked to see that."

"You are right," Marco said. "Nothing is nice dead. Even how much I have hunted I always feel sorry for what I kill." He hurried to add a more pleasant note to the conversation. "But when the meat is roasting on the fire and you are hungry and you get that nice fresh smell—ah, then it is something else."

"And you still think you're going to get that deer after what I told you?"

"Now I am positive." As they turned to walk back along the road Marco reached forward eagerly and touched his finger to the collar of Elena's coat. "So positive I am that I will invite you to eat a steak with me next week. How do you like that?"

"We'll see," Elena laughed.

Giustina sat in Federico's armchair near the window watching across the street. Every time she saw Angela pass and hesitate before Emilio's house she leaned forward, her expression tense until Angela went on again. From the cellar came the muffled sound of voices and the clinking of tools as the mechanics worked installing the oil burner. The house was cold. She sat huddled like a mummy in the folds of Federico's heavy overcoat, with the chill penetrating her meager frame. Even when Elena entered the room she didn't get up.

"You throw them the bills?" she asked. "You tell them is finish the wait and is right now we want be pay? This bizaness have the big heart! Sure, be good to the dog and he bite you hands. What they say?" She leaned forward in the armchair again.

"They were scared to death," Elena said. "In fact they were so scared it looks to me that Emilio better—— What are you watching, for heaven sake? Why don't you come into the kitchen instead of sitting there shivering? We'll light the gas stove until the heat comes on again."

"Here! Look what I watch. That lilla bum from up on the hill. She no want leave Emilio alone. She wait and she wait and she no go away. Pretty soon I go over there and I tell her something myself."

"Where's Emilio?"

"He there, inside. Where you think? He no want come out. She no see the car because is in the garage and she wait for him come home. Is make me dishgust see girl run after man like that. Live like the animale and act like the animale."

"You mean Emilio is home and he knows Angela is there on the street and he won't come out?"

Giustina nodded her head and snickered. "Is what I mean. Was no for that. Was no I am sure Emilio want have nothing with her, I show you how I run over there and pull the hair from her head. Pthew! Vergogna! Girl make such dirty shame from herself."

"Then if it's like that," Elena said meekly, "you don't have to worry. She'll go away by herself after a while. Come into the kitchen before you catch a death of cold."

Giustina allowed herself to be coaxed away from the window. In the kitchen Elena struck a match and lit the oven of the gas range. She unbuttoned her coat and stood silently before the stove warming her hands. Giustina went to the cellar doorway and called downstairs, "Federico!"

"Watch you wants?"

"You tell the men hurry up. Is too extraspensive the gas in the kitchen for keep warm." She turned to Elena. "I no hear before. What they say up on the hill? What you tell me for Emilio?"

"Nothing. I just gave them the bills and said we wanted the money and they looked scared."

Shortly before dusk a blue sedan with official gold lettering on its sides pulled up in front of Emilio's house and Enos Wilkins, the village peace officer, got out. He was a bulky man with a healthy complexion from being out of doors all the time. As Emilio greeted him and showed him into the waiting room, he removed his cap which also served as a repository for cigars and papers and flopped gracelessly into a chair, unbuckling the leather belt of his holster. He passed his hand through a wiry crop of red hair. "What's up, Doc? Mad dog around or something?"

"First a drink," Emilio said. He didn't bother with glasses, handing Wilkins the bottle. "Drink up, Wilky! A drink to an up-and-coming medical man. Yes sir, boy. Just ask Doc Stone, chief at the hospital."

"That's all right. Here's to you, kid." The policeman

swallowed a mouthful of whisky. He gazed at the label
with a nod of satisfaction and set the bottle down. "This
why you called the wife in such a rush and made me jackass over here without my supper?"

"Like hell," Emilio said. He pulled a chair over and sat
down beside the policeman. He pounded his fist into his
palm. "Now get this! There's a hobo living up on the hill
with Giuseppe. You never saw the guy. But I swear if you
don't help me get the sonofabitch out of here you'll be
coming around to pick me up for murder." He went into
a dramatic account of what had taken place down in the
swamp. "—and me there with Doctor Stone and this guinea
snotty as hell, just like he was the game warden. And not
only that. He got all the other wops worked up. Pretty
soon, by Jesus, they'll be running the town."

"What you expect me to do?" the peace officer said,
calmly picking his nose.

"Listen. That buck had three slugs in his side. He didn't
go very far. Sure as you're a foot high they'll have it quar-
tered and home just as soon as it's dark. But that's not the
point. The hell with the goddamn deer now. But that
begging hobo grease ball who thinks he's a wise guy!"
Emilio paused. He leaned closer to the policeman. "Now,
all you have to do is pay a surprise visit up there around
ten o'clock or so. Somehow, you got wind of a deer being
shot. Don't worry, you won't find it. They'll have it shoved
under the floor of the chicken coop or someplace. But you
know it's there, understand? Then you lace into them.

Make them jump right out of their boots. Pick on the strange guy, the hobo. That's all. By the time you get out of there they'll all be so yellow-livered scared I wouldn't give a nickel for that hobo's skin."

The policeman rubbed his knuckle against the side of his chin. He bit the end off a cigar. He seemed doubtful. "I don't know. I get a lot of complaints about those Eyetalians hunting out of season but I never yet caught them with a damn thing. If I wanted to do the game warden's work, it wouldn't be up on the hill I'd look. You can bet your shirt on that."

"You don't get the idea," Emilio said holding back his irritation. "I don't care a rotten fig for the deer. Christ, do I look like I got to go out poaching to eat? All I wanted was to get Doc Stone a shot at one. But the law! That's the thing those wops are afraid of. I'm warning you. If you don't do as I tell you and that hobo gets the run of things up there, then you'll have some real trouble on your hands."

"I still can't see it. It don't sound kosher. I just can't size the thing up."

"Jesus Christ! Once I ask you to do me a favor and you balk like I was asking you for a thousand dollars. I'll put it this way. A deer was shot down in the swamp. I'm making the complaint. Now you go up there and raise hell about it. There you have the whole thing perfectly legitimate and in line with your duty."

"In that case I'd call the game warden and have him take care of it."

"All right," Emilio said. "If that's the way you want to act——"

"Don't get sore. I was only kidding. Okay. Just throw a scare into them so they bounce that hobo out on his ass. I'll make it good. Boy, you never saw me when I really go to work."

"Now you're talking. Here, kick another shot down," Emilio said. "Tell you what! We'll meet at the drugstore at ten. Maybe I'll go along. Why not? It 'll be dark. I can stay in the car and maybe listen. Hell, that's an idea."

However, at ten o'clock it wasn't so dark any more. The moon came up and a million stars appeared in the sky. Emilio insisted on going along just the same. The druggist wanted to go too, only the policeman wouldn't have it. Elena sat quietly at the soda fountain.

As they got into the car and started up the hill to Wop-Roost the policeman said, "What's the matter with Elena? She didn't say a word tonight."

"Search me. Maybe she doesn't feel well. Anyway, I have enough trouble with my own women without worrying about her."

"Say, what's this I been hearing about you and Giuseppe's daughter?"

"You're crazy like everybody else. I took her out driving a couple of times and now I can't get her off my neck." He laughed. "Jesus, the poor kid waited for me a couple of hours this afternoon. She marched up and down in front of the house, and I couldn't go out because the old lady was watching over in the window. Finally she took the bus and went off to town. Probably to look for me at the hospital. Well, she'll go to the movies by herself. I don't know how I get mixed up in these things."

"I know. Those knockers she got! Lord, they'd like to slap you right in the face."

"You're telling me? But I'm telling you, boy, that's dangerous stuff. Before you know it you're hooked."

Now the car rumbled past the first groups of shacks. Dogs started to bark and came running to nip at the wheels. Faces of women appeared at the windows and children in nightshirts stood on their beds to witness the event of an automobile in the night. Emilio slouched low in the seat. He whispered, "Pull over to the side. I'll keep out of sight. Remember, just barge in there sore as hell. By the guilty look on their faces you'll know the deer is around someplace. Give it to them hot. Push the law stuff and make it look like that big bastard was responsible for them getting into trouble."

As the car came to a standstill a little beyond Giuseppe's house the policeman said, "I couldn't see inside. Funny nobody comes out."

"Go ahead. Stop using your head so much. Rush right in."

The policeman got out of the car. He chased off the dogs smelling around his feet and strode boldly across the stretch of ground separating the house from the road. At the door he paused for a moment. Then he banged with his fist and pushed the door open. "Where you guys got that deer!" he shouted. But he stopped dead just within the room. His jaws fell apart and his eyes swelled to huge orbs of astonishment. There, only a foot from his face, was the deer, trussed up by its antlers to the ceiling. The room wasn't quite high enough and the deer seemed to be sitting on its tail, with its neck and head jerked upward to the sky.

"Well I'll be a——"

The Italians were sitting around quietly in a haze of tobacco smoke and the odor of perspiration and garbage burning in the stove. With the exception of Vincenzo they were all there. And they were still and mute, like so many mourners sitting up with a corpse. Nick hobbled out of a chair and offered it to the policeman. "Allo, Meesta Wilk! We glad you come. Sit down."

"Like hell I'll sit down. Of all the goddamn open-faced—— This takes the cake!"

"Is make nice sight for the game warden tomorrow morning, no?" Nick said, not paying attention.

"What you mean? What you guys trying to pull?"

"Nobody is trying to pull anything," Marco said. He came forward and stood in front of the policeman. "It is just that in the morning the game warden will know who he is trying to find around here for breaking the law and killing the game." He counted on his fingers, "Doctor Emilio Gardella, the man from the drugstore and the big Doctor Stone from the town. Makes a nice combination for him."

"Who 're you?"

Beppo sprang from the floor. "And is the Italianos on the hill what kill the deer and leave them to die in the swamp!" he cried.

"And is the Italianos you watch and the game warden watch like the hawk and everybody have the suspish!" Luca shouted.

"Shut up, all of you!"

"It is not now the time to shut up," Marco said. "You are the man here who the people pay to keep the law. Your job depend up here just like down below and it is now you who will call the game warden and it is us who will make the complaint. Italians! Poor! Afraid to talk! Now we will see who is afraid to talk. This deer was killed. We saw how it happened. And here is the proof. You will go now for the game warden, or I will go down to the village and telephone myself."

"Who the hell you think you are, trying to tell me what to do?" But the policeman's voice was flat, the fire going out of it fast.

"Is no you bizaness who he is," Nick said. "He my friend and he Giuseppe friend and he live here in Giuseppe house. Is you bizaness call the game warden."

"And come back here and find the deer gone? Oh no. I'm not that dumb. You won't pull that stuff with me."

Marco bent low to heave the deer with his shoulder and lift the antlers from the hook on the ceiling. "We will put him in the car for you. Giuseppe and me and Tony, we will

go along. You do not have to be afraid for the deer or anybody up here to run away. Down in the village is where
they have to be afraid."

"Now wait a minute," Wilkins said, backing away toward
the door. "Leave that deer hanging right there. Let's get
this thing straight."

"There is nothing to get straight. Just do your work to
make the report and we will take care of everything else."

"But goddamnit, I don't want to see you fellows or anybody else get slapped with a five-hundred-dollar fine and
maybe go to jail."

"We no afraid the fine or the jail," Nick said. "Tony, help
Marco put the deer in the car."

"No," the policeman said. "You'll only make a lot of
trouble and put yourselves in bad with everybody. That's
no way to act when you got to live in the same town with
other people. Keep the damn deer here. I never saw it.
Never even heard about it. Looks like a good eating deer
too."

"With the horns like that!" Beppo said. "Tough bastich
like him is just like to eat you shoes. What for we gonna
have the worry keep him here?"

"And if they keep the deer here, it is just the same like
they break the law," Marco said. "You know that."

"Now that ain't so. I never bothered these people. I just
keep my eyes open and do my duty. They never had no
trouble with me and I don't want to make no trouble for
anybody, up here or down below."

"That's right," Giuseppe said, getting up enough courage to speak for the first time. "Meesta Wilk, he never bad with us. He just come by in the car and he look. But is for that he is the police, no?"

"You fellows do what you want. Just keep everything quiet and I won't open my mouth to anybody. What the hell's the sense making a big stink and causing a lot of hard feeling?"

Marco was silent. Nick held up his hand. "All right, Meesta Wilk. Is for you we do this. But is no for the people what shoot this deer."

The policeman's cheeks were burning. He grasped hold of the doorknob, smiling, trying to appear cheerful—a good sport. "Just keep it under your hat," he said as he pulled the door open. But when the light of the room was shut away and the cold air hit him he gasped and went rushing to the car. He flung himself inside, gripping the steering wheel savagely and grinding his heel down on the starter.

"What happened?" Emilio asked in a hushed voice. "I couldn't hear a damn thing."

"Shut up, you punk, before I ram my fist down your throat!"

8

THE LAST BUS from town sped along through the night, the driver's eyes sleepily focused on the white flare of the headlights. The bus was almost empty. Angela sat up front near the driver, her hands folded in her lap, her feet pulled under the seat to receive the warmth from the heater. Her knees showed. Several times the driver turned to smile lazily and allowed his glance to linger further down. Angela paid no attention. She smiled back mechanically and then the smile was gone and her lips became serious. The blond-haired driver vanished from before her eyes and there was only the darkness outside the window to her right, the dull hum of the tires and her thoughts.

To the rear of the bus sat an elderly couple, awkward in their Saturday night clothes, the man with big clumsy hands and knobby knuckles, the woman without make-up, her face severe. Both of them asleep with their heads nodding and swaying. The driver watched the old couple in the mirror above him. He said to Angela, "How was the show tonight?"

"It was all right," Angela said and lapsed back into silence again.

He tried a different tack. It wasn't that he wanted to talk particularly, but talking gave him a good opportunity to look at her legs. "Where's the boy friend? Mean to say you went to the movies all by yourself?"

"That's what I mean," Angela said. She had no further comment, turning away again.

"Tough," the driver said. "Now if it was my night off. I mean if I didn't have this lousy job, you can bet you wouldn't have to go to the movies by yourself. What about tomorrow? Tomorrow night they got a different picture. What d'ya say?"

Angela didn't answer. The bus was approaching the village and she had her face pressed close to the window, watching the dark silhouettes of the houses flash by. Before she had been calm, but now nervousness crept into her manner. The program from the movies was in her hand and she raised it to her lips, biting the edges. As the bus rushed past Emilio's house and she saw the lighted windows she got up quickly and held on to the iron support near the door, waiting for the vehicle to come to a stop. She stepped down to the sidewalk and the driver said, "Well, you don't have to act so high-hat. I was only asking." He rammed the gears again so that the old couple in the back jumped in their seat, startled.

Angela waited until the bus rounded the turn and disappeared toward the far end of the village. It was late. Even the drugstore was closed. She looked up and down to make sure no one was about and then started quickly along the sidewalk to Emilio's house, running on tiptoe up the front steps. As she was about to knock she heard a voice from inside which she recognized as Elena's and backed away down the steps again. She hurried across the street and found shelter in the entrance to a grocery store where she could watch and wait out of the cold.

The bus came by on its return trip to town, headlights flashing against the buildings. Angela huddled out of sight. In the dark she tried to see her wrist watch. She held the cheap, silver-plated timepiece close to her eyes and finally was able to distinguish the hands. A quarter to twelve. She stepped from her shelter for a moment and peered through the night to the top of the hill. There were lights still. Here and there a phosphorescent glow from a window. She was unable to see her own house but she knew there was a light burning there too. She backed into the doorway again, frightened, shivering, frantic at the passing time.

In the waiting room Emilio paced back and forth, one hand deep in the pocket of his dressing gown and the other holding a cigarette which he kept tapping into an ashtray on the magazine table. Elena sat in one of the armchairs, hatless, her coat open and listening. Her face was pensive, quizzical, the delicate curve of her chin drawn against her knuckles as Emilio said, "All right. They beat me. They put it over. The big guy did it. I can see them now, laughing at me. Okay. I was a damn fool. I figured wrong. But something'll happen up there. They'll need me. They'll need me bad. . . ." His voice heavy, the edge and the sharpness gone out of it. He was a little boy who had gotten a beating and talks, brags without really believing what he says. He crushed his cigarette into the ashtray and stood with his elbow on the mantel of the fireplace, staring down at the hearth and running the toe of his slipper along the pencil lines of cement between the tile.

"Yes," Elena said. "That's the way you feel now. But if something really happened up on the hill and they needed you, even the one you hate most, you know what you'd do."

"You're a fool! What does the suffering of one patient mean to me? When I was an interne at the clinic you think it was always the serious cases that got the most attention? Like hell. It was the patient whose family could afford to slip one of us a couple of bucks now and then. It took me a long time to get wise. I had it knocked into me. I had a lot of things knocked into me. Things that you and people like you never realize."

He moved away from the fireplace and closer to his sister. He struck a match to another cigarette. "In medical school I was in with the crowd. Fellows from the best families. Why?" He made the motion of rubbing his thumb against his index finger. "Money. That's why. My father had money. Ability didn't mean a damn thing. I was one of them. I acted like one of them and I spent money and they accepted me, in spite of my name. But there was another guy. A thin, dark-looking kid, the son of an Italian pharmacist, working his way through school by washing dishes in a cafeteria. He was the typical wop and he was poor. It didn't matter he had more in his head about medicine than the rest of us put together. He was out in the cold. Just a little wop medical student destined for some little wop community in some little town. I learned all right. The hard way. I learned if you're an Italian you've got to become an American and you've got to become successful. All that crap you see in the movies about the self-sacrificing doctor —try and find it when you get out in the world. Money is the thing that counts, and money excuses everything."

"Then what about Doctor Stone? You say he has taken an interest in you, has a professional respect for your ability. How do you reconcile that to your theory? Certainly he can't expect to gain anything by cultivating your friendship."

"How do you know?" Emilio said. "I'm a good doctor. A damn good one. Maybe Stone can use me." He clenched his fist. "Stryker, Goldsmith, Stone! I got it in me to be a better doctor than any one of them. Stone knows it. That's why he's interested. But this much I know: I'm going to get to the top of the heap. Who cares how you become successful so long as you get there? I know the things I want. How I'll live. The people I'll associate with. The girl I'll marry.

Why should I deny myself these things because I happen to be the son of Italian immigrants? Why should I suffer because of the accident of birth? Not me, sister!"

Elena leaned forward in the armchair. "What do you mean?"

"Just what I said."

"You talk as if you had the whole thing all figured out. How can you be so definite? Better men than you have set a course for themselves and failed. I don't suppose this could possibly happen to you?"

"Oh no," Emilio laughed, "not the way I'll go about it. What you need is guts. If you got guts you get anywhere you want to go. You just wait and see. Why, I bet my kids'll grow up to think their ancestors came over on the Mayflower."

"That'll be funny. Olive-skinned Yankees." Elena smiled. "But maybe Doctor Stone can do something about that too."

Emilio became annoyed. "You and your wise cracks! Come on now. It's getting late. I want to get some sleep."

Elena got up. "I wish it could all sound as good to me as it does to you. Maybe you can tell me why, with all the young medical men in town, Doctor Stone should develop a sudden interest in you?"

"Jesus Christ, I told you!" in exasperation. "Because he saw me work. Because he knows what I can do. Does that satisfy you? Now go home to bed."

When Elena had gone Emilio flopped into the armchair

left vacant. He sat motionless for a time with his legs out-stretched, his hands on his knees and his head thrown back. He sighed. He ran his fingers through his hair and reached over to the table for a magazine. After staring blankly at the cover, he threw down the magazine and got up. He was about to switch off the lamp when a knock came on the door. He turned around in surprise. The knock came again and he saw Angela's pale, frightened face appear.

"Angela!"

He rushed over and drew her into the room, shutting the door quickly. "You little fool you! What made you come here at this time of night?"

Angela couldn't speak. Her face was red and swollen. Tears glimmered in her eyes and her teeth chattered. Emilio rubbed her hands. He went over and pulled down the window shades. Then he poured a little whisky into a glass and forced her to swallow. "I couldn't make it this after-noon. Come on, try and pull yourself together. That was smart, coming here now. You almost ran into my sister."

"Nobody knows where I am," Angela managed to say. Her chin dropped forward on her breast. "I tell you it wasn't my fault," Emilio explained. "I just couldn't make it. The trouble with the deer. That bastard hobo up there. Don't start crying, will you!"

Angela trembled. Little reddish spots appeared on her face and hands, brought to the surface by the cold and her emotion. "I waited for you. I went to the hospital. I was all over. I had to come here. I couldn't go home without seeing you."

"All right," Emilio said. "I'm sorry. Now powder your face and straighten your hair. You must go. They might have seen you from the house."

"In a minute," Angela said. But she made no motion, standing there with the helplessness in her eyes. Emilio tightened the knot on the sash of his dressing gown. He walked away from her, across the room and came back again. His hands reached out in a desperate appeal and then fell to his side. "Oh hell!" He put his arm around her shoulder and kissed her. "You're acting like a little kid, Angela."

"I'm not acting like a little kid," Angela said. "I'm only acting human. If you felt the way I felt all afternoon you would act the same way too."

"It's not that. I'm just trying to be sensible. At the present time I can't afford any complications. I have too much to think about. You should try to understand."

"You don't care about me any more. You're trying to get rid of me," Angela sobbed.

"I am not."

"You are too."

"Look," Emilio said. "Tomorrow's Sunday. You go home now and get a good night's rest. We'll spend the day together. Call me in the morning after church. I'll meet you someplace."

"Promise?"

"I promise."

Angela smiled. It came slowly at first but it was a real smile and with her tear-stained face made her more childishly beautiful than ever. Emilio kissed her again. He opened the door a crack to look across the street and then, squeezing her hand, allowed her to slip past out of the house.

On Wop-Roost the rejoicing, the excitement of victory was over. Beppo, Luca and Tony staggered off to their own shacks, each a share of meat under his arm and stumbling through the darkness under the soddening effects of too much wine. Luca dragged a sack containing the intestines of the deer which he was going to feed to his pigs. Inside the house Marco sat near the stove, piling in wood to burn up the hide and the antlers and the rest of the evidence. A window was open, and yet there was the gagging stench of singed hair and burning flesh.

Giuseppe quietly wrapped a hindquarter in newspaper to hang out in the chicken coop. Over on the couch Nick lay sprawled, humming to himself in a half sleep. He struggled to a sitting position and grinned sheepishly into the empty wine glass still in his hand. He laughed. Catching sight of Marco across the room, his laughter increased. He got to his feet and tottered over, gathering Marco in a tremendous hug. "Meraviglioso! Never before I have such a good time like tonight. Like the top from the world I feel. I feel I go right down now and kick in the ass the mayor."

Marco wormed out of his grasp. Now Nick stood in the center of the floor, his arms folded and gazing at Marco in admiration. His fat body swayed like a ship riding at anchor. "I tell you what I gonna do," he said, smacking his fist into his palm. "I make you partners from me. I make you partners from Nick—the best tree specialist doctor in the whole world. How you like that?" He opened his arms again, but Marco ducked aside and he fell headlong on the cot. The legs sagged and the cot flattened to the floor.

"You drunk, crazy drunk!" Giuseppe shouted.

Together they helped Nick back to the couch. Marco pulled off his shoes and stretched him comfortably. But Nick's feelings were hurt. "Go to hell everybody! Smart man like me need nobody for partner. I make plenty money by myself and then you be sorry." And he even had an idea for a new kind of tomato plant he was developing. A tomato different from all the rest—yellow and big, with a taste all its own. He wanted to get up again and show Marco the seeds he had in his suitcase under the couch.

"You go to sleep now," Marco coaxed. "Tomorrow we will talk. I have an idea too."

"You sure is a good ideas?" Nick said suspiciously.

"There is no idea better than this one I got."

"We make plenty money?"

"Hell with the money," Marco said, turning serious. "People like you and me and Giuseppe, we will never have money. But we will have a good life. We will work. We will produce. The things we know we will use. And that is better than the money which makes the Italian rich and his happiness poor."

Giuseppe stood with the wrapped quarter of deer slung over his shoulder, listening. Nick said, "And I can send for the wife and the kids? Is no good a man stay too long without his wife."

"If everything goes right," Marco said. He winked at Giuseppe. The eagerness in Giuseppe died. It was all a joke then. He glanced at the alarm clock on the table and went out to the chicken coop. Nick rose on his elbows. "You no tell nobody this ideas. They steal it. Just like they steal from me my work and my trees. Is just for us. You proomise?"

When Giuseppe returned he found Nick asleep and Marco fixing the legs of the cot. He closed the window and threw some more wood into the stove. He gathered the empty glasses from around the room and placed them in the sink in the kitchen. He came out of the kitchen again and flopped into a chair at the table, yawning and stretching his arms over his head. He picked up the alarm clock and wound it slowly, looking at the time and shaking his head. "Twelve o'clock pretty soon now and Angelina no home yet. Ah, how is the life easy for the girl today. She go out. She dance and do what she please. At seventeen she more free than the woman what is marry. I remember in Italia when I was young. My sister. If she stay out just one hour after the dark, come such a wallop from my father she holler to the next town. And when she go out to the dance sometime, and when she go to the church, is always somebody there to watch—my mother, my sister from my mother, or somebody. Never the girl go anyplace alone before she get marry. And after is the husband to look out. But here!" He shrugged his shoulders to emphasize his lack of comprehension. "Here I the papa of the family. But what I know? My dog I know more what he do than Angelina. If I ask some lilla thing, right away she get up in the air. Is no more the respect for the papa. Is no more the family, close—everybody together. Maybe is better this way. But sometime it make me feel sad when I think I am papa and is just like I have nobody and I never get marry and I am all alone. . . ."

Marco set the cot upright again and sat down. He loosened the collar of his shirt and ran his hand around the back of his neck. He didn't answer for a moment. He studied the narrow boards of the floor, worn smooth and light, and the nailheads showing through. There was silence, the crackling of the fire in the stove and Nick snoring away—dead to the world. Finally Marco said, "It is the change. It is the New World. Many of the things we remember from the old life we must forget. They have no place here. No more the long hours of work from when it gets light in the morning to the night when it is dark. Work is good but it can kill a man too. Here you do your work and you have time to think and the time to enjoy other things too. There is more balance to the life. And the woman is free, and that is another good thing. Over there is the family behind, pushing and forcing the marriage they think is best. Here the girl marries the man she likes—and the happiness is greater because it is free."

Now Marco nodded his head and smiled. "That is good." But then he held out his hand in a leveling motion. "Slow, slow. Not too fast. For the Italian there is a wonderful life in America. But he must go easy. If right away he tries to tumble down everything, then he is lost. He is not strong any more. America is not for him. He will die—like the Italians I have found all around me. . . ."

Giuseppe listened quietly. After a silence he said, "Beppo, Tony and Luca. And even Vincenzo. They more happy than me. They no have so much to trooble their head. They work lilla bit. They hunt. Go to hell everything else and what the other people think down below. They no give one damn about nothing so long is something to eat in the house. 'Guinea, Wop-Roost? So watch you want? You want I shoot myself?' Me, I am no the same way. I worry for what I no onderstand. I try to change—make myself more like American people. Is Angelina I have to think. Is no nice for young American girl have papa old fashion with ideas from the old country. People laugh. In the school the kids make joke with her. It get me all mix up. Like you say, is something dying inside. I no feel strong. I no feel sure any more. And is very bad this. Because how a man gonna live a good life when he no can tell what is the right way for him to be?"

"There is only one way to be," Marco said, getting up from the cot and kneeling on a chair in front of Giuseppe with his elbows on the table. "There is only one thing that counts. That is to never forget you are Italian and to never be ashamed. People like you and me! We will never become real American. There is too much behind for us to change. But we can be a part of America. We can give to it just as much as the people who call themselves Americans because it is here where they were born and they have the flag waving outside the window. We bring the blood and the life and the energy that from the beginning made this country something. All the rest of the people who come from the other side of the world! Italian, Frenchman, Polish, Swede—there is no difference. They all belong to America—and the Italian just like anybody else. We marry and the blood is in our children. Our children marry and there is the mixture of the blood. And the race becomes stronger and better. In the end you are important to this country as much as the policeman who was here tonight." Here Marco extended his finger and shook it slowly. "But if the minute you land here you want to rush to become American, then little by little you kill yourself—and you cheat the land that gives you a home because what you brought with you from your own country to make it richer and better you have thrown away and forgotten. You have come just to grab. There can be no happiness, no real joy of life for the man who is traditori to the past. To the present he gives nothing. And the future will never remember him. . . ."

Giuseppe's lips parted into a smile. The smile broadened

into a grin. He started to say something, but Marco held him to silence. "So it is like this: When the fellow who thinks he is American calls you a wop you look at him right in the face and tell him to go to hell. When an Italian calls you a wop you spit on him. And the worry will be gone. And there will be no more confusion. When there is something to decide you will know what to do."

"Salamangonia, you right," Giuseppe cried. "Is already I feel better. Like new man you make me feel. I think I give you job stay here and make me feel good." He got up from his chair and started to pace back and forth across the room, with his thumbs jerked into his armpits and grinning in a satisfied way which made Marco laugh.

Just then there came the sound of a hand on the door-knob. Marco stopped laughing. Giuseppe's face became stern as he watched the door open and Angela enter the room. She walked in with her head lowered and then looked up startled as she saw her father standing before her. But it was only a momentary suggestion of feeling.

Immediately her face became expressionless again, doll-like, waxen and beautiful with her luminous eyes and deep chestnut hair and full red lips. Without even bothering to look at Marco or notice the bloodstains on the floor or the heavy, oppressive stench still lingering on the air she started toward the door of her own room.

"Wait a minuts!" Giuseppe said in a voice filled with un-accustomed authority. He grabbed the clock off the table and shook it under her nose. "Fine time. Fine time for young girl come home. Where you was all day from after lunch to after now? Talk. Open you mouth."

Angela tried to pass but Giuseppe remained, blocking her way. There followed a slight quivering of her lips, an angry glare, and she pushed her father aside and ran into her room, slamming the door. Giuseppe took several quick steps to follow. Then he stopped with his hand on the door-knob. His shoulders sagged and his hand fell to his side.

9

FOR GIUSTINA Sunday had a special appeal. Whereas during the week she got out of bed grumpy and with mind only for the business of the day ahead, on Sundays she greeted the morning cheerfully and was even pleasant to Federico. She would waken long before rising time and lie there in bed thinking of the hours before her. Again and again she saw herself getting out of the big Packard before the austere masonry of the church, Emilio on one side and Elena on the other and the people of the village smiling to her and nodding their heads. And then the solemn entry into the church, the genuflection, the seriousness and the importance of it all. It was always the same, and yet always different and wonderful to think about.

At seven o'clock instead of thumping Federico with her foot, she nudged him lightly until he woke. Then Federico

knew it was Sunday too. He got up yawning, his flannel
nightgown swathed around him so that he looked like a
veiled monument, his mustache bedraggled and the iron
hair curling out at his chest. He shuffled downstairs sleepily
to run the bath. In another few minutes Giustina followed
to scrub his back which he couldn't reach himself with his
short fat arms and they were both closeted in the bathroom
for a half-hour or so, scrubbing and cleaning in preparation
for church.

This morning, as Giustina entered Elena's room to waken
her, she was surprised to find Elena already up and sitting
in front of the dresser, combing and brushing her hair,
smiling happily at her reflection in the mirror. A narrow
strip of sunlight, falling across the room, caressed the side
of her face and heightened the glow of color there. Giustina
stood behind her daughter, fixing her own hair, picking the
hairpins from between her thin lips and impatiently poking
them into place. Elena said, "It'll be another lovely day
today. A few accidental days like this and then the nasty
cold and the wind again and the snow. I wish it were summer." Her lightness changed into a little scowl of dis-
content.

"Please, you call Emilio now," Giustina said. "You wake
him up. Otherwise we be late."

Elena applied a touch of lipstick. She pressed her lips
together to smooth out the color. "Why do we always have
to bother Emilio? Let him sleep. You know how much he
likes to go to church. Every Sunday it's the same thing.

You have to drag him along and he just sits there bored to death and yawning his head off. You think it's good. It's bad because everybody notices and I've even seen Father O'Malley give him dirty looks. It's enough trying to keep Papa awake without worrying about Emilio too."

"You make mistake," Giustina said stubbornly. "Emilio like to go to church with his mamma. He know is my pleasure. You wake him up."

"You call him. He may be in one of his moods this morning and I feel too good to get into an argument."

"Why?" Giustina asked quickly. "Something happen last night? What they do for the deer?"

Federico passed the doorway dressed in his black Sunday suit, on the way down to the cellar to shine his shoes. He heard his wife mention the deer and stopped. He edged into the room and stood stiff, awkward, with his neck rubbing the starched collar of his shirt as Elena said, "Nothing happened. Only he made a fool of himself and the policeman too. They practically told the policeman up there to go and jump in the lake. You call him if you want to."

"On the hill they tell the police jump in the lake?" Giustina said in amazement.

"That's what I said."

Giustina couldn't believe it. She looked to see if Elena was joking. "Jump in the lake," she repeated dumbly. "They tell Meesta Wilk jump in the lake." She brushed past Federico and hurried down the staircase. Up in the bedroom they could hear her at the telephone, waiting for

Emilio to answer. Federico watched Elena as she gathered the dress she was going to wear over her head and let it come down over her slip. He stuck out his chin in a grimace to express bewilderment. "Is true, this?"

"Of course it's true. They got the deer and Emilio and the druggist can't do a thing about it without getting themselves into a mess."

Federico's cheeks puffed and he clamped his hand over his mouth to stifle a guffaw. He tiptoed close to Elena, his eyes shining humorously. "I betch," he said. "I betch was the big fellow bum responsible for this."

Elena didn't answer. There was something of amusement on her lips. Federico nodded. "He nobody monkey, that man. Five minuts after I see him I know." He pointed to his temple. "Got plenty inside here. And you see how he save Giuseppe from the tank? Something inside here too," lowering his hand to his heart. "Remember me myself when I was young."

While the family was seated at breakfast Emilio came in. He seemed a trifle pale, his face drawn and hollows under his eyes as though he hadn't slept well. He took his place quietly, picked up a spoon and began to dip into his grapefruit. Giustina reached across the table to touch his hand. He pulled away. And when she started to pour out against the Italians up on the hill he snapped her into silence. "For God sake, shut up about them! Give me a little peace." He turned from his mother to glower at Elena and continued to eat his grapefruit.

"Happy family," Federico said in disgust. "Everybody talk so nice. Everybody love everybody else so much. We go to church. We make the show. In the basket a dollar. And we fool nobody. Bah! The money and the show and the try to be high-class people. What it all count when is the family inside like this? I watch the man, the poor bastich who work for me three dollar a day. I watch him with his wife and the kids. I—I——" Something sudden and unexpected came over Federico. His voice caught and he got up from the table.

"What's eating him?" Emilio asked in surprise.

"What's eating you?" Elena said. "What's eating Mamma? What's eating everybody in this house? I don't know. Don't ask me. But it's getting me too. That's all I know."

"Me you blame for everything!" Giustina shrieked. "Me who make life so easy for us!"

"Oh, I'm not blaming anybody. I'm simply saying there's something definitely wrong in this family."

"What's wrong, smarty?"

"You for one thing," Elena said, looking straight at her brother. "You're all wrong and you know it."

"Nuts, will you!"

Federico came through the kitchen again with his hat and coat on to go to the garage for the car. "Finish with the argumento," he said. Then he added with sarcasm, "We go now to kneel down and pray. Maybe for one dollar extra God he do something special to fix up the trooble in this house."

They were coming down along the road from Wop-
Roost, the poor Italians. To church, to meet in prayer with
the other Catholics of the village, poor and well off alike
to gather for one hour together beneath that vaulted dome
of silence and offer up incantations for the promise of a
better life—the believers and the difficult-to-believe, giving
their pennies and their nickels and dimes, and some their
dollars for the Promise.

The women waddled along the road in front, clinging
to the hands of the smaller children, while the others ran
on ahead to meet companions at the door of the church.
The men walked behind. They were all there, except Nick,
who never went to church, and Luca, who had gotten up
with a heavy head. All of them, including Marco, dressed
in a clean shirt and wearing a tie and Nick's overcoat with
the crinkly black fur collar. They were laughing, still talking about the deer and the expression on the policeman's
face when he opened the door. They stopped for a moment
while Giuseppe grabbed up a rock and went chasing after
his dog to scare him from following down into the village.
He came back slapping his hands and they moved on
again. Beppo said, "Now we will see Emilio. We will see
how the fine gentlaman doctor feel this morning. Ho, ho!
The wop, Italiano on the hill! He no can pull the double-
cross, hey! Is just to wipe under the feet. Salamangonia, we
good like anybody else. No, Marco?"

"And because you are good like anybody else, you live

in a shack with tarpaper on the outside," Marco said, turning to look back along the road.

Beppo's jaw fell. The others looked questioningly. They were a little doubtful as to whether or not to take this as an insult. But the beginning of irritation was there. A little distance above, the shacks spread out, dark and ugly, patched on the top of the hill like a congealed mass of tar and rubbish and rotting lumber. Marco's gaze remained fixed for a long time. The eyes about him followed in line. He shook his head. "The Italians dirty! They live just like the pigs! The people who say that are right. Except Giuseppe here, you all live like that. You, Beppo. You, Tony. You, Vincenzo. Tarpaper, junk, the window broken and the patch with cardboard, the chicken coop made from boxes, the fence around the garden from bedsprings from the dump. Even in the old country you do not remember living like this, with no respect for yourself and your family and your children who will grow up and mix with the other people."

There was no answer. Heads averted and eyes downcast. Beppo kicked a stone with the side of his shoe. Tony, swimming in an overcoat miles too big for him, poked his finger into the bowl of his corncob, while Vincenzo sucked his cadaverous cheeks. Further along one of the women waved and they started walking again. "I cannot understand," Marco said. "Or the Italian is like the family down there, or I find him like this—worse than he was before."

Vincenzo pulled a twig from the branch of a dead tree,

snapped the twig between his fingers and threw it away.
"The talk is fine," he said peevishly. "Poor like we are! The
talk for respect! The children! Tomorrow my Alfonso he
find a girl and get marry. You think he live with me? You
think he gonna bring his wife to live up on the hill? You
crazy. Is just me all alone and Maria. Go to hell what come
after we gone. In the church we think maybe is something
Up There. But is more probabla only the worms in the
ground. We live best we can. Tomorrow?" He jerked his
hand into the air.

"Then to live like this, it was better if you never came
here," Marco said. The words came from his lips slowly.
There was nothing of anger or reproach, only the under-
lying conviction of his thoughts. "It is the Italian like you
who helps make people like Doctor Emilio and the man
from the drugstore and everybody else who thinks like
them."

Marco brought the conversation to an end as they neared
the main street of the village. They turned south, away
from the stores, past low dwellings neatly arranged in a
row, the lawns stretching out in front and the flower beds
with the fallen leaves of autumn raked over them. They
passed the firehouse, a broad, flat building of yellow stucco
with a little tower on top, like a bird coop, for the siren.
The doors were open and the gleaming red fire engine
shone through the sunlight. Several of the volunteers,
young men of the village, were up on the truck polishing
away at the brass and nickel. They raised their rags and

nodded pleasantly as the Italians went by. Marco nodded too. "It was a good idea, the idea of Sunday," he commented. "There is no rush, rush like on the other days. Everybody takes it easy. Everybody has a little time to say hello and be nice to the other fellow."

A short distance further along they turned right, into a narrow side street, and the church came into view. The chapel of gray-brown stone with its broad slate roof at a precipitous tilt and surmounted by a simple cross. The turreted window of stained glass in front depicting the Shepherd and his flock. The parish house to one side, also of gray-brown stone, but built low and flat and severe. "Ah!" Marco said. "It is a beautiful church for a little village like this."

"Is beautiful all right," from Beppo. "Cost plenty. Plenty. The stone. The roof. The fancy windows. This place to walk from the street. Flagstone five inch thick." He pointed along the walk past a statue of the Madonna to the heavy-paneled door of the chapel, now opening and closing to receive the worshipers. "Special kind oak. Poogh! Was big contract all right. Too big. Somebody make plenty money, you betcha."

Tony, Beppo and Vincenzo crossed over to the other side of the street to join the women and children. Marco and Giuseppe lingered behind, watching the automobiles pull up and the occupants get out to stand for a moment as independent little family units and then merge with other groups, bowing, smiling and moving along the flagstone walk. They saw Federico's hearselike Packard go past, turn around and come back again, parking at the end of the line, and Emilio as he jumped out to open the door for his mother and sister.

Marco laughed. He indicated Giustina, who held her head high and her lips tight as she moved through the congregation with her son on one side and her daughter on the other. "She is very proud of her work." There was the quick, ready-made smile and the aloofness when she passed the Italians which made Elena uncomfortable and embarrassed Federico, who waddled along in the rear like a dressed-up duck. But Giuseppe paid no attention. He was watching something else.

"Look, Angelina over there!" he said, nudging Marco. She was standing off to one side with a girl and several boys of her own age. They were talking and Angela pretended to listen, but her eyes followed Emilio and there was a breathlessness in her gaze almost painful to watch. For a moment it appeared certain Emilio would go by without turning his head. In Angela the emotional suspense became something hypnotic. Then Emilio turned. It was simply an involuntary action of his head. But it was enough. Immediately the color rose in a crimson flush to Angela's cheeks. Her bosom heaved and her lips parted into a smile of relief as her companions snickered to each other.

"The young people suffer when they love," Marco said. "It is a part of the romance. The pleasure must be mixed with pain or they have no way to know when they are in love." He scratched the back of his ear and chuckled. "I remember the first time when I was in love. A big fat woman would come every week with a little donkey and a wagon to sell things like pots and pans for the kitchen. What a size! But I thought she was beautiful—an angel. And I would stay awake in the night wondering how I was going to keep alive until the next time she came. I was only fifteen and she was more than thirty. But that made no difference to a love like I had in my heart for her. Then she killed me. I was dead for more than a month. She married the man who made cheese in the next village."

Giuseppe laughed a little. He looked for Angela again, but she had disappeared into the crowd forming a funnel at the oak doorway to the chapel. Now the cars stretched in a lifeless line across the street and there was only the hurried footsteps of the stragglers. Giuseppe's small, shrunken face gave evidence of hidden anxiety, and then his features fell away into the mildly querulous expression that was characteristic. "We go inside now?" he said.

"Just as well," Marco answered. "On such a morning it would be nice to take a walk and see the village and the country around here. But we will go in. The first time I have been inside of a church in ten years. Maybe it will do good—who knows?"

As they crossed over, Giuseppe said, "Is like I feel myself—who know? Only after my wife die I start to go to church here. One hour on Sunday I make the pray. Is for her. Now the time has pass. Is hard remember any more exact what she look like. The picture in my head change alla time. Sometimes is like Angelina and sometimes is a face like the Madonna with the Baby. But in the church I can think and I try remember. It make me feel better."

Then they were kneeling together in the last pew, near the door, Giuseppe lost like a little child behind the backs of the worshipers bent before them, and Marco straight, his eyes fixed over the bowed heads to the altar where the priest in his holy vestments mumbled Mass. There were the intonations of the choir boys and the heavy silence, the odor of mold from the walls and of incense from the altar and the rose-colored light as it filtered through the stained-glass windows. Across the aisle, toward the center of the congregation, Marco saw Federico. Next to him, Emilio, his gaze wandering, now fixed on the flickering candles beneath statues of the saints, on the transverse beams of the ceiling and the luminous particles of dust floating in a shaft of sunlight. Then there was a gap beside Emilio, the mother, hidden from sight. And then Elena. He saw her in profile, the pallid gold of her skin, the curve of her lips and chin and the straight, delicate line of her forehead as she knelt with her eyes closed and her head inclined forward against her clasped palms. He continued to watch her. Later, when the service was almost at an end, she turned to look around and saw him watching.

As Marco and Giuseppe filed out ahead of the others they came upon the druggist standing in the entrance, holding his hat in his hand. He seemed excited and anxious to go in, yet he did not enter beyond the first door. The sight of Marco startled him, causing little purple veins to come into prominence on his nose and cheeks. He didn't know whether to smile or scowl. However, when he saw everybody rising into the aisle he moved further inside away from Marco and Giuseppe, who stepped out into the cold morning air, laughing to each other.

The druggist nodded politely as members of the congregation greeted him. When he saw Emilio he waved. "Morning! Morning!" he said quickly to Federico, ignoring Elena and Giustina in his excitement. He took hold of Emilio's arm and led him on ahead.

"What's the matter?" Emilio asked, but the druggist wouldn't answer until they were away from the front of the church and standing off to one side by themselves. "It must be important! Doctor Stone called. He's been trying to get you all over. He wants to see you. This morning. You're to call him at his house."

"No!"

"I swear to God," crossing his hands over his chest. "Spoke to him myself. He couldn't get you so he called me at the store."

"What did he say? What did he want?"

"Search me. But he was nice as pie. About fifteen minutes ago. I left a kid in the store and came running over myself. I was going right inside and tell you but I didn't know if it was all right."

"Jesus!" Emilio cried, clenching his fist. "Come on, let's go." He hurried to where his mother and father were waiting near the car. He could hardly speak. "Doctor Stone called," he gasped to Giustina. "Telephoned he wants me to call him right away. At his house," pulling open the rear door of the Packard. He looked around. "Where's Elena?"

"See! Over there with Maria," Giustina said fiercely. "Look how she talk those people after what they do."

"So she talk," Federico grumbled. "The Italiano people they dogs, she no can talk?"

Emilio shrugged his shoulders. There was too much on his mind now to worry about Elena or the Italians up on the hill. He even forgot about Angela, who stood on the opposite side of the street, waiting. "Get in. Get in. Elena can walk home," urging his mother and father into the car. He took the wheel himself while the druggist walked around to sit beside him. As the huge vehicle jumped forward he slapped the druggist's knee and grinned.

Elena saw the car go down the street and turn through the village. She looked after it somewhat puzzled, excused herself and moved apart from the Italians, slowly following the flagstone walk away from the church. She saw Marco and Giuseppe and her face lighted into a smile again. Giuseppe had his dog under his arm. He had taken off his belt and Marco was fastening the buckle to the little hound's collar. She walked over. Marco put his cap in his pocket. Giuseppe also tried to remove his hat and hang onto the dog at the same time, while the animal struggled against his chest and stretched to lick his face. "Lilla salaman-gonia," Giuseppe said proudly to Elena, "is no use I holler him to stay home. He follow me every place. Bad. He get kill someday by automobile like that. I have to keep tie, I guess." He put the dog down and held onto the belt.

The dog nosed against Elena's coat, sniffing into the soft fur. Elena drew aside, laughing. She reached down and patted the little brown head and the soft, pendent ears. Then she turned to Marco. "I guess you won about the deer," she said, half in a joke and half seriously.

"I told you what would happen if the policeman come," Marco said.

Giuseppe added quickly, "We sorry. Up on the hill we no want trooble with Doctor Emilio. But was no nice him send the police scare everybody." He started to fumble, all mixed up. "Was no nice," he repeated.

"No," Marco said in a firm voice. "We are not sorry—we are glad. And the next time it will be the same, until your brother learns it is not because he is a doctor that he can treat the Italians like dirt just to show himself different in the eyes of the other people."

"You should set yourself up as a dictator," from Elena in mild amusement; "you seem to have gotten such a hold over these people."

Giuseppe was a little embarrassed. He saw his friends passing on the other side of the street and he pulled on the dog. "You 'scuse me, please. Is the wood to chop this morning. Is many things for me to do." However, he lingered on, waiting for Marco.

Marco's eyes went from Giuseppe to Elena. He looked down at the dog and then over at the Italians going by. "You go, Giuseppe," he said. "I will come soon. I will be up in a little while."

10

"SO YOU THINK I am trying to be a dictator?" Marco said. By some unspoken consent they proceeded to walk slowly back along the narrow street, passing the church again where the crowd had thinned and only a few members of the parish remained, chatting the Sunday-morning gossip. They strolled beyond the church where the street rose in a slight incline and curved gradually away from the village through the green, pine-tipped acres of a tree nursery. Elena hadn't answered. She was smiling to herself. "They seem to be willing to do anything you say," she said finally. "And when they want to talk you are right there to put the words in their mouths."

"A dictator," Marco repeated. "It is a word when you know what it means you do not use so easy. I can tell you that." He watched Elena out of the corner of his eye. He tried to be strong in what he was saying, but the mirth on her lips made it difficult. "What is so funny?"

"I don't know. Everything seems funny to me today. It's just one of my funny days. Tell me," she said. "Why did you come to church? You don't believe what goes on in there any more than my brother does. But you came. Why?"

"For many reasons. To see the people of the village. To see how the church works in this country. And for a reason like the one of Giuseppe. He goes because he can think and remember his wife. I have things, too, I like to remember. It is easy there in the quiet."

Elena had no comment. Marco continued: "It is not a wife. I have never had a wife. It is happiness I try to remember. Like the man who grows old looks back to when he was young. For somebody my age that is bad. But——" He ended suddenly with an indefinite motion of his hand.

"I can't understand," Elena said. "I still can't understand what made you come to America." Now the humor was gone and she turned to him questioningly, her lips calm and her eyes seeking an answer somewhere in the strained perplexity of his brow.

"Because I thought I could find here what was no longer possible for me over there. A free life to live without anybody to tell me what to do and what to think. And land. To have land that is mine to plant what I want and to feel with my fingers. Simple. So simple it is ridiculous to you who have never lived on the other side——"

Marco paused. "Go on," Elena said. He studied the callous on the palm of his hand. "In Italy when the family owns land it is rich. But when the land is gone then the family becomes poor. My father was a good man and he did what he could for his family. But for the land he was never able to manage. There was always some piece to sell for money he needed. And when my brother, the oldest one, got married he took the best share. And after, the share for my brother Julio. Then my father died, and my mother. There was still two more brothers to take care of. What was left for me? A little patch of ground, the worst of a big farm that once I remember was the best anyplace. It could never keep a man and his family. Work? What kind of work for a man like me will pay him enough to live and buy land besides?"

He heaved a sigh which ended in a smile. Then he closed his fist. "That is one of the reasons. The other is something else. The story of the end of life for the free man with his own ideas in Italy. The story of do and think like one individual or rot in prison. The story of that word you like to use which used to make me crazy but now only hurts me to talk about. And with this, what I used to hear about America. The people who came back and could not stay more than a little while. The money here. The land for everybody. I got drunk with America. New people. From every place in the world, helping to make this country grow. It made my head go around, the idea of America. My share of the land I sold for the trip. Ah, when the boat sailed from Napoli that day it was like dying. But there in front of my eyes was the wonderful picture of what I was going to find. . . ."

Marco opened his coat. He turned the pockets of his trousers inside out. "Six years. Seven. Eight. I cannot remember any more. A hobo. A bum on the road, moving around, trying to find the real America. From a farmer I learned to work in the factory on the sewing machine. I run away and I always come back to it again. That goddamn sewing machine! But the Italian. The good Italian I know from the old Italy. The simple man. The honest man. What has become of him? The man without the sickness to make more money than he can use? The man with the pride in his work and the happiness in his family?" He pointed across the village to the rising heights of Wop-Roost, the shacks visible through the winter trees and remaining shacks even with the enchantment of distance and the gold of the morning sun.

"There are your real Italians. Your unspoiled Italians," Elena said.

Marco shook his head. "To live like that they were better off never to come to America. They just make a show in front of the people who look down on top of them. It is like they want to prove they can be like the Americans think they are—miserable, all living together on the top of a hill, doing nothing to change, thinking only of dogs and hunting and maybe work now and then when they need food. Because in Italy only a man with property could hunt, over here they think they are rich because the land is open and they can carry a gun. They are good people but they are fools to themself. That is not life. That is the animal who is satisfied today and never thinks for tomorrow. That is not the happiness of a man who builds a house and says to himself, I have built a house and I have built it beautiful and strong and my children will want to live in it after me. Or of the man who plants a field and is careful what he plants because he loves the ground and he knows there are others who will love and care for it when he is gone. That is happiness—if out of yourself you give something that will last when you, the man, will be no more. That is the real work of the Italian in America. When he is like this he becomes the true citizen."

They had walked some distance now along the street bordered by evergreens on either side. Elena hadn't noticed the cold before and now she trembled a little. They turned to go back. An automobile came tearing along from the village and Marco held her arm as they stepped aside to let it pass. Elena felt the power of him. There was the immensity of his hand and the smallness of her arm beneath his fingers. It seemed all he had to do was draw his muscles taut and lift her into the air like a doll. "If you stay. I mean—if you don't go away—what will you do?" she asked.

"I will work," Marco said. "If up on the hill they can find work, I can find it too. Here I feel there is some hope, among these people who do not know the American sickness of money. I will teach them to live better and with respect for themselves. We will get together and fix up the houses, one by one, and clean up the ground. Instead of ten dollars for a new dog and twenty-five or thirty dollars for a new gun, we will use the old gun and the old dog and there will be a pump in the kitchen and a toilet in the house. They will change if there is somebody to show them, because inside they know that the way they live is not the best way."

Now Marco faced Elena squarely. "But these are peasants, men of the ground, and they need the ground to make their life full. It is not the pick and shovel, or the digging wells, or the selling ice, or the day of work at anything that will make them happy. They need the earth to turn and the things to grow and the feeling inside they are doing what they were meant to do, and what their fathers did, and the fathers before that. It is not possible to throw everything away in the time of one life and have a satisfied man. Not possible. He will die just as sure as when he cuts his veins and the blood goes out. He will become hard. He will become bitter. And no matter how much his success, he will fail. You know I am right. You know, if you ever thought about it at all. By your own family you know. . . ."

Marco stopped talking. His hands dropped to his side. The nervousness, the tensity left him. He searched into his pocket for tobacco and paper and rolled a cigarette. Elena tried to answer. She tried to form words, excuses, arguments pounded into her head by Giustina, but they caught on her lips. She was only conscious of Marco as he swallowed a breath of smoke—conscious of his face, the broad forehead, the dark hair receding slightly at the temples. Out of her confusion she said, "I don't know. You mean Emilio and my mother. I always had a feeling they were wrong but I never knew why. But they know what they want, and that gives them something people like me haven't got. You see, since a little girl I never knew what I expected out of this world. The things other girls craved didn't impress me very much. It was the same when I went to college. I never felt at home there. But I liked fussing around with my father's business and taking care of things for him. Anyway, it gave me the feeling of doing something. That's not what I mean, though. I don't know what I mean. The things you've said. I've thought about them, and I haven't. Like vague dreams in the back of your head which never come clear and you never mention to anybody. . . ."

They were walking along the main street of the village now, in silence, approaching the bend where the stores crossed in front of them. Almost together they stopped. Elena extended her hand. There was the heightened color of her cheeks and the confusion still in her eyes. "I'm sorry. You see, I feel kind of foolish not being able to talk and say exactly what I mean. But that's the way I am, I guess."

"It is enough for me just to have somebody to listen who understands," Marco said, holding her hand for a lingering moment. He wanted to say more. But now, after the long silence between them, even the sound of his own voice seemed out of place. He only smiled and pressed her hand lightly before crossing to the other side of the street and turning into the road leading up the hill to Wop-Roost.

When Federico's big Packard pulled away from the church Angela followed slowly. Her companions came running and wanted to walk with her, but she told them she was waiting for her father and they went on ahead. Then she started again, taking it easy, pacing out the time she figured it would take Emilio to finish whatever he had to do with the druggist and get back to his own house. At the fire station one of the volunteers called, "Hi there, Angela!" and she stopped. The boy was under the engine, peering out at her from the side of one of the wheels. He grabbed hold of the wheel and pulled himself up. He was dressed in a canvas jumper over his good clothes and stood there, eying Angela with a good-natured, know-it-all smirk on his face and wiping his hands on a piece of mechanic's waste. "Where you been keeping yourself? We ain't seen you around."

"Don't be a stoop!" one of the fellows on top of the truck said. "Where you think she's been keeping herself?"

"I've been looking for a job, smarty," was Angela's reply. She stiffened her body and tilted her chin at an angle calculated to place years of experience behind her.

"I suppose you need company to look for a job?" came from above.

"Aw, cut it out," the boy in the jumper said. "Hey, Angela, there's a dance tonight at the Valley Rest. We got Gladys and Viola. We'll pick you up, huh? What do you say?" His eyes were big with eagerness.

Angela turned away indifferently, staring back along the street. She saw the Italians coming along and her father in front leading the dog. She moved alongside the truck and into the building. "Let them pass," she said, motioning with her finger to her lips. All the heads stretched in amusement. The boy in the jumper took her by the waist, led her around the fire engine and out of sight. They remained quiet within the building while the volunteers lined up out front, their work temporarily disrupted. He continued to hold his arm around her and there was a vapid, embarrassed smile on his face. He squeezed harder. Angela didn't move, but when his hand reached down a little further she pulled away and said in a harsh whisper, "Cut it out or I'll smack you." Outside she heard the Italians pass. Just to be funny one of the fellows called, "How's it, Giusepp?" Then her father's broken reply, "Is pretty good, Freddy. How everything is by you?" and she blushed.

"So what do you say?" the boy repeated anxiously when the Italians had passed. "We'll have some fun. I got my brother's jalopy. Huh? Come on, be a sport."

"I'm sorry. I can't. I'll be busy."

"What the hell she want with the Valley Rest?" the smart aleck said. "She wants the Swan Inn. She wants a guy with a satchel, old enough to be her old man."

Angela walked off with her head in the air. "Kids!" she said in contempt. When she was out of range of their jibes she slackened her pace again. She opened her handbag and rummaged for a nickel, closing the bag again and holding the nickel in her hand. Nearing the drugstore, her steps quickened and she moistened her lips. As she entered the air of thrilled expectancy fell away when she found the store empty and only the druggist, in his starched jacket, leaning against the counter reading the headline of one of the piles of Sunday newspapers.

"Hello, Angela," the druggist said. Then he remembered he had something to feel sour about and blinked a few times. "Damn smart that hobo your old man took in. A wise guy. One of these days somebody 'll push his face in. Sorry I didn't take a whack at him myself that night when I had the chance."

"You're lucky I was up there," Angela said quickly. "He wanted to go right down and get the game warden. On account of me he didn't."

"On account of you! You mean on account of a hundred and fifty pounds of eating venison. Don't kid me. Any time those paesanos let that much meat out of their hands! Goddamn, it was a nice buck. Makes me boil every time I think of it."

"Just the same you can thank me," Angela said. The druggist shook his head. He coughed and went to the door. He returned, wiping his mouth with his handkerchief and mumbling under his breath. Angela studied the buffalo on

the nickel in her hand, walked to the rear of the store and
into the telephone booth.

"Hey," the druggist called. But just then a customer came
in for newspapers. "And a pack of Camels, George," the
customer added, sitting down at the counter for a little
chat. The druggist got the cigarettes and rang up the money
in the cash register. "Lovely day," he said. "Spring in January. Then tomorrow snow up to our ears. Didn't use the
chains once yet this year. You?" He looked over the customer's head to the telephone booth, watching Angela
through the glass door as she held the receiver to her ear,
waiting for an answer at the other end of the line. "A car
is a damn nuisance anyway," he continued, "but when you
got to use chains it's double-up. Christ, I hate them."

The customer hung on. Angela came out of the telephone
booth with the nickel still in her hand. She walked past
the customer and outside. The druggist raised a shoulder
and pursued his conversation about skid chains. A little
later Emilio came in. He had on a newly laundered shirt
and there was a trace of the talcum powder he had dabbed
on his face to freshen up the early-morning shave. He
winked at the druggist. "I got in touch with him," he said.
Then he joined into the discussion, at the same time picking at his fingernails with a tiny pocketknife. When the
customer left he asked, "Did you tell Angela I had to go
to town?"

"I didn't get a chance," the druggist said. "She'll be back.
You can tell her yourself."

Emilio was annoyed. "Hell, on purpose I didn't answer the phone. I got enough to worry about right now. Stone had to go out all of a sudden on an important call. The nurse said I'm to be at his house in about an hour. Christ, I'd like to know what he wants. Before I was all worked up. Now I feel nervous as a kitten."

"Maybe he wants to fix it for you at the hospital?"

"Can't be. He was too anxious to get hold of me. I could tell by the way the nurse spoke. It's something else. I got a sneaky idea. Then maybe it isn't that at all. I wish it was over."

"What the hell you care what it is," the druggist said, "so long as he needs you for something. Listen. You're in good with that nitwit you were telling me about whose father is a big shot at the club. You're sitting pretty with Hazel Lambertson. That fixes you over there. All you need now is a push from Doctor Stone and, man alive, you'll be right on top of the world. With your looks those rich dames 'll be flopping all over you. They'll invent a sickness just to have you feel around. And you're worried?"

"I'm not worried. Just a little nervous, that's all. I can't help it. You go along for a year wondering what's what and then all of a sudden things start to break. It scares you just a bit. Last night on account of that sonofabitch and that deer I was down in the dumps. I thought everything was queered. And now the picture looks better than ever." He paced across the floor. "I'd give fifty bucks right now just to know what Stone's got on his mind."

The druggist reached under the counter for a special bottle hidden in a special place away from his wife's prying glance. "Here, have a snort. Go ahead, take a good stiff slug. You'll know what it's all about soon enough. Just don't act like a chicken. You got the stuff. And Stone knows you got the stuff. So that makes him a smart guy, but it doesn't make you a goddamn fool. Understand? Nobody does nothing for nothing, specially in that crowd. It's all politics. If he got something up his sleeve, use your noodle and figure out where you come in." He raised the bottle to his own lips. "Down the hatch! Brrrr—what lousy whisky. Well, you're on your way, kid! Only don't forget George when you come rolling by in a big Cadillac with a chauffeur and a fat cigar in your mouth and your nose up in the air like if everybody else smelled from limburger."

Emilio laughed. He glanced at himself in the mirror behind the counter and adjusted his tie. The druggist drew his attention to Angela coming from across the street. "You talk to her," Emilio said. "I'll duck in the back. Tell her I had to rush to town to see Stone and I don't know when I'll return."

"Like hell. Don't mix me in this. It's your business. I'll go in back and you talk to her yourself."

When Angela opened the door Emilio greeted her in a hushed voice to indicate that the druggist was listening at the rear of the store. He explained about the telephone call from Doctor Stone. "I'm sorry, Angela. But this is something big, something I can't afford to miss up on. You know what it means to me."

Angela smiled. It was a smile from her mental picture of Emilio's success and her part in that picture too. "I'll go with you," she said excitedly. "I'll wait in the car outside."

"Don't be silly. I may be fifteen minutes and I may be all afternoon. How do I know?"

"You could leave me at the hospital. I'd stay there in the waiting room until you picked me up."

"It's impossible. I haven't the faintest idea when I'll be free. Can't you understand?"

The expression on Angela's face changed to one of perplexity. She tried to understand. "If you did happen to get tied up like you say, all you'd have to do is call me and I'd take the bus home. Maybe it's nothing important for today and then we'd have the afternoon together like you promised."

Emilio sighed wearily. "Let's not argue, Angela. You can't come with me, that's all there's to it."

"Because you're going someplace else. You have another appointment. You think I'm a fool. I know."

"I think you're becoming a pest."

Angela looked straight at him. Her eyes grew moist but there was determination in them. "All right, go to your appointment. You think I need you? You think I have nobody else to go out with? Just now I was asked to go to a dance at the Valley Rest tonight. Just a few minutes ago. And I'll go too."

"With who?" Emilio asked scoffingly.

"Wouldn't you like to know?"

"Oh, go anyplace you want to go, will you—only leave me alone." Here Emilio turned suddenly and went out of the store. Angela rushed to follow. But when she saw him head down the same side of the street to his father's house she stopped, waiting for him to look back. As Emilio disappeared, it seemed she was really going to cry. Then she sniffed a quick breath and bit the corner of her lip. The druggist came out and stood in the doorway, watching. Angela glared at him with contempt and walked away toward the other end of the village again.

11

SUNDAY AFTERNOONS, with the heavy meal of the day over, Federico devoted to catching up on affairs of the world. This meant he usually plunked himself down in his armchair with the front section of the newspaper and, after struggling over a few of the important captions, fell asleep. The paper fell to the floor. His head drooped and he began to snore—slowly at first, rising in gradual crescendo, until he came awake with a start and the process began all over again.

For a long time Elena had been silent, kneeling on a chair, with the rotogravure pages spread before her on the dining-room table, listening to the ceaseless chatter of her mother about Emilio and the wonderful progress he was making with Doctor Stone, Hazel Lambertson and the rich people in town. Now Giustina had exhausted herself and sat quietly at the table with the sewing basket before her darning a pair of Federico's socks. But the shrewd, satisfied smile was there still and Elena knew she was embroidering in her mind the dream of Emilio's future. She looked at her father and waited until his snoring reached the breaking pitch once more, then coughed and rattled the pages before her. Giustina's eyes raised questioningly. Elena said, "Just to forget about Emilio for a little while and come to something else: What are we going to do about the Smith farm?"

This interruption proved distasteful to Giustina. It was like suddenly being reminded of losses in the midst of a calculation of profits. "What we can do?" she said sharply. "You put the advertise. You put in the hands every real estate. Just was bad invest. How we was gonna know when we give Smith the mortgage they leave everything go and we get stuck with the land what is no more worth like before? You. Federico. You say rent, keep, keep—is always worth something. I say, cost money, we sell. Better we lose something instead pay tax and have the headache try to rent when is nobody want the farm around here any more."

Federico opened his mouth wide in a lingering yawn which ended in a nod. He picked the corner of his nose and rolled what came out between his thumb and forefinger. "If was my father have such a farm like that, you sure I no be here in America today." He smiled to Elena. "You know what it mean in Italia have such piece property? It mean you somebody. Have maybe ten, fifteen people work and when you pass they take off the hat. Is all right. Was nice I remember be big proprietario. Now with Mussolini is everything upside down, I guess. But before was nice. Here the small fellow jealous because you got what you got, and the big fellow he try to take it away from you. Everybody like the wolf—spit and show his teeth. Ah, Dio, Dio! Sometime I think place like Smith farm, raise the vegetable and the chickens, mind my own bizaness—is sure much better life than have the worry alla time for we got now."

Giustina listened. Her body swayed to the singsong of her husband's voice. "Very nice," she chanted. "Very, very nice when Emilio say to the people from the cloob, my papa he chop the ground and my mamma she carry the vegetable in her skirt. Very nice. I am sure they say, is wonderfool, very cute have mamma and papa like that."

Federico caught his daughter's eye. He raised a chubby hand and let it fall on his knee. "Is like the filosofo talk to the wall, I talk with that woman. Only one thing she have in her head," closing his eyes once more.

Elena didn't answer for the moment. She leaned forward pensively, her elbows on the table and her chin supported. Then, when it seemed the subject was gone from her mind, she said, "We ought to run that farm. It's just going to ruin. We ought to make it produce something."

"Watch you say?" Giustina snapped.

"I said, something should be done. As it stands, the place

is a total loss. From a business standpoint it could be made to pay for itself. That's what I said."

"The daughter like the papa. One just the same from the other. Pretty soon you want we sell the house and take a shack up on the hill. Instead do clean, nice bizaness, we plant cabbage ar.d on the back of the donkey you bring the cabbage to sell. Emilio, he close up the office, raise the pigs and the cows. I suppose is this watch you like, no?"

Elena sprang away from the table, the color mounting in a rush to her cheeks. She stood in front of her mother with her fists clenched. "Emilio! Emilio! That's all I hear in this house. How wonderful he is. What he's going to do. It remains to be proved. He hasn't done anything yet. He hasn't even the good will of the few patients he's got. But what about me? Where do I come in? He asks for anything and he gets it. I ask for nothing and I get nothing. What about the money you've spent on him you haven't spent on me? My share—where is it? The money he squanders that I helped earn?"

There was a dead silence. Giustina paled. Federico began to squirm uncomfortably. "Elena. Please. Don't get excite."

"Keep quiet," Elena said. She wheeled on her mother again. "I don't want anything. I'm not worried about my share of the money or what belongs to me. But once in a year when I have something to say I want to be heard and not have the example of Emilio up before my face all the time. I don't care what Emilio wants. I only hope he gets

it. But I know that I have done more for this house than
Emilio probably ever will do. And if I took that farm?
Even if I gave it away, it would only be a small part of
what's coming to me——" Here her voice caught. She was
trembling. Her eyes flooded and she rushed from the room.

Giustina grabbed up her darning and sewed away at a
furious rate, her lips tight together, the needle flying beneath her fingers. "Now the farm she want to give away."
Her voice was a squeak, the scratching of chalk on a black-
board. "She crazy. She sick in the head."

"Shut up!" Federico roared, his mustache bristling like
the hair across a dog's back. "Shut up now!"

He went after Elena and found her down in the cellar
sitting on the crate near the furnace. She was sitting with
her legs crossed and her arms folded, staring ominously at
the blank concrete wall in front of her. Federico approached cautiously, clicking his tongue in a kind of sym-
pathy mingled with disapproval at her loss of temper.
"Whatsamatter, Elena? Why you get all upset like this?"

"Oh, I'm fed up," Elena said. "I'm sick of everything.
There isn't anything decent and real in this family. It's all
money and getting ahead and trying to be something we
weren't meant to be. It's too much." She passed her hand
across her forehead.

"Watch you want to do with the Smith farm?" Federico
asked suspiciously.

"Nothing. Just forget about it."

"Come on," Federico said, taking hold of her hand, "talk with you papa. I no bite you. Where you go this morning after the church?"

"I went for a little walk with Marco. Why? Don't you think I'm old enough to do as I please?"

Federico had nothing to say.

"Why couldn't we run the farm?" Elena said. "What's so disgraceful about being a farmer? Is it any worse than being in the contracting business or selling ice? That's what I can't understand. It makes me furious. Why shouldn't I like the idea of having a farm to look after? What were you on the other side? A businessman, I suppose? Then I can't help it if there's a feeling inside me for something that has nothing to do with sand and gravel and making entries in a ledger. Something that would give a little personal satisfaction for a change. Oh, what's the use. . . ."

Federico was silent. He twirled the end of his mustache, looking away from Elena to the other end of the cellar. There was a suggestion of pain in his features but of tiredness, too, more than anything else. "Even if I'm not to be considered here," Elena went on. "Even if my feeling and desires are to be sacrificed for the financial success of the family. Forgetting me entirely. Just suppose you had to hire Nick and a couple of men to fix up the orchards and the vineyard, men to repair the house and barn—how much would it cost? Plenty. You know it. But if we let out the farm on a share basis—the rent to come out of the produce, along with a percentage of profit? Assuming failure, and we had advanced a few hundred dollars for expenses, the work accomplished would come less than if we had to have it done ourselves. That's what I was trying to say."

"And is the people on the hill who will do this?"

"Why not?" Elena said quickly.

Federico stroked his chin. "But after what happen the deer, is like to put one stick dynamits under this house." He paused to reflect. "For propozish is no too bad. What we can lose? Nick, I no have much confidence. He stuck once before with idea like this. Giuseppe, Luca, Beppo— hummm! Is the farmer in the blood there all right. I know that. But how they work together, now, after so many years everybody for himself? Is hard to say. But this big fellow, Marco! If he stay. From him I feel maybe they have good chance for success.." He nodded his head slowly. "Why I think this, I no can say. Is a man like one stranger to me, and yet is no like stranger at all." Then a thought made his eyes grow wide. "But plenty broccoli! Ah, is a plant I always like—the broccoli. And the American people they eat like anything. They think is something new, special kind vegetable they make discover here. Poogh! The broc- coli I remember from—I don't know how many year."

"And the pears," Elena said, "and the apples and the grapes! Why, the grapes alone bring forty dollars a ton. And there's corn and potatoes and cabbage, and crops like celery and Brussels sprouts which go late into the fall. You'd have something to ship to market almost the whole year round."

"Is no such a bad propozish," Federico repeated. Then he clicked his tongue against his cheek. "Emilio. You mamma. Is there the trooble."

"We'll tell them. We'll come right out with it. After all, we have something to say here."

"No," Federico said. "Is no right now the time. We wait. Lilla by lilla I talk to you mamma. From the side of the money I think I catch her. Emilio?" He scratched the side of his neck where his jowls came down almost upon his collar. "With Emilio I have to talk the language plain."

At that very moment Emilio was listening to language, if not spoken plain, at least precise in every detail of pronunciation. He had been waiting for the past half-hour in the spacious study of Dr Stone's home. Here was just the sort of study his mind had always associated with a man like Dr Stone. English in effect. Oak paneling to the ceiling, finished dull, amberous and restful. Books, hundreds of them properly arranged, the bindings uniform and expensive. The fireplace simple, a part of the wall. A conical bronze lamp on a pedestal which threw light to the ceiling and diffused it evenly. The desk, large yet delicate in design and catching the tone of amber too. The chairs and the flooring and the soft rug beneath his feet—everything to his own taste.

When the nurse opened the door and Dr Stone entered, Emilio had exhausted his examination of the room and was standing at the window with a highball glass in his hand,

gazing through the curtain at the broad terrace in front of
the house. He set the glass down on a little wagon bar arranged with an assortment of bottles and a silver bowl
for ice. He smiled, one hand extended, the other adjusting
the double-breasted coat of his dark suit.

"I'm sorry, old man," Dr Stone said after a vigorous
handshake. "I really am. Thought I'd be back at least two
hours ago. Been all the way down to Ardensburg. Mrs
Carter. An old patient of mine from town here." He spilled
a little cognac into a glass and swallowed it down. "A
shame to keep you waiting like this. Did you eat? I told
Miss Perry to fix a tray for lunch."

"Thanks," Emilio said. "When I stopped by the first time
she told me you wouldn't be back for a while so I took a
run over to the hospital. I had to make a couple of phone
calls and grabbed a bite while I was at it."

"The phone was right here," Dr Stone said reproach-
fully. He yawned. He stretched his arms high over his head.
"A little stiffened up today. But that bit of hunting yesterday was just the thing for me—just what I needed. By
George, in my sleep last night I'll wager I shot that deer a
hundred times! Ah, there's a man's thrill! Gun to shoulder
and a big buck deer running across your field of vision.
Believe me, Gardella, when you get my age all the thrill
and excitement left in the world is in hunting and fishing.
The quick shot and the tumble of game. The sudden yank
at the line and the rod bent in half. These are things which
never pale. They follow you to the grave. Man stripped of

all the varnish of civilization—returning to the basic, the elemental."

"You're right there," Emilio said. "Only I certainly feel I owe you an apology for yesterday. That one episode makes me look like a damn fool."

"Nonsense. It was sort of amusing to come to grips with brute man. The tall one! You had your spunk to face him. But for our guns he might have wiped out the three of us. Splendid physiological specimen. When you think of it it's a shame the price we of our society have to pay for progress of the mind. But that's the way it goes, I guess."

Emilio nodded. He picked up his glass again. Dr Stone was silent for a moment, as though pursuing his thoughts on the degeneration of Man. He looked at Emilio and coughed to clear his throat. "Well, Gardella," he said, pacing slowly toward the other end of the study.

Emilio nervously lit a cigarette. Dr Stone turned around, head lowered, studying the design of the rug. Then he looked up. He picked a pencil from the desk and held it loosely between his fingers. "Two men," he said in a simple voice. "Two of us in the same profession. You at the beginning of the climb, young, eager, ambitious, filled with the ideals and aspirations of your calling. Me at the other and with everything behind, the illusions, the disappointments, the successes—pretty nearly everything. I wonder if we could really talk and understand each other, you and I?"

"We might try," Emilio laughed.

"I've always kept my distance with young medical men," Dr Stone continued. "The gap of experience is a difficult thing to bridge. And never, wittingly, have I tried to influence a man to alter the course he has set for himself. Life's too short and each of us must learn in his own way. That's why I find it difficult to be blunt in this matter I want to talk over with you. Understand what I mean?"

Emilio nodded. Dr Stone dropped the pencil. He molded the air with his hands. "Let's try to be absolutely disinterested. Let's look at the thing from a purely professional angle. I've discussed you with Stryker and Goldsmith and both of them agree that you've shown amazing competence in handling this case you have with us now at the hospital. It wasn't just accident. You've got everything you need right in the tips of your fingers. You show promise of becoming one of the best obstetrical men I've ever seen—and that, coming from an old war horse like me, is something of a compliment."

"Thanks." Emilio blushed a little. "Now," Dr Stone went on. "Please. What I'm driving at reflects in no way on your integrity as a doctor. We'll set all that aside and talk like two intelligent humans. I don't know what your plans are for the future, or what you intend to do exactly in the way of medicine and surgery. It's none of my business. But here's the situation I am facing at the moment." Emilio accented the pause with an understanding movement of his head. Dr Stone said, "In the past I've had certain cases —all of us have them here occasionally—when I wished to

God I had a man of your ability I could depend upon. I mean it, seriously, instead of those quacks down in the city who give themselves over to the wholesale performance of illegal operations because they couldn't possibly make a living any other way——"

Here Dr Stone glanced from Emilio to the trim manicure of his fingernails. "Yes," Emilio answered. Now the feeling of nervousness was gone and he puffed calmly on his cigarette. "Frankly," Dr Stone said, "I'm right at this moment in the same sort of situation. Yes, it is a situation. Of course I might just wash my hands of the thing or let someone else worry about it. But that's not me. I'm a human being too, as well as a doctor. Here is a girl from one of our best families. A love affair. The thing went sour and she comes running to me. Why, man, I held that girl on my knee when she was a child. Her mother and father are among my best friends and patients. You just don't rear up on your dignity and shout that much-maligned word 'ethics' and allow the girl to turn in despair to a professional abortionist. That's too simple. Life is not that easy. It's the way of the hypocrite who reflects the attitude behind laws which pontificate that a girl has no business to sleep with a man, much less get herself caught. What the deuce kind of sexless humanity made possible these rules we are governed by, I don't know. But there it is. . . ."

Emilio crushed his cigarette into the ash tray, watching the smoldering ash and a thin film of smoke which vanished against the ceiling. "And you want me to—how would you put it?—you want me to perform this operation?"

"I wouldn't want you to do anything you don't want to do. You know your mind better than I. I've simply taken you into my confidence. I assure you, one way or the other, it will not affect my personal feeling toward you. It's a case I just can't trust in my own hands and because of what I've seen you do at the hospital, I thought I'd mention the matter, that's all."

Emilio's lips curved into an almost imperceptible smile. "Who is the girl?" he asked casually.

"That depends," Dr Stone answered. "Under the circumstances I couldn't very well permit myself the liberty of telling. But she has an independent income of her own, left by her grandmother. If you feel justified in helping this girl, I would suggest—let's say a fee of five hundred dollars. How does that strike you?"

"I see it only in the light of being able to do something for you," Emilio answered. "Money can only be a secondary consideration at best."

"Put it any way that suits you. Still, five hundred is a nice piece of change. And one never can tell what might develop from this. After all—I mean there is a distinction—society girl as against poor immigrant laborers for patients. You know what I mean, Gardella."

"I know what you mean all right. When do you want me to take the case?"

"Sooner the better. Tomorrow. The poor girl is on the

verge of hysteria. I think it's advisable to get it over with as soon as possible. You haven't a nurse, have you? No? Well, I think we can take care of that without any trouble." He went over to the movable bar and poured two drinks, handing one to Emilio. "You've taken a load off my mind, old man. I can't tell you how relieved I feel. This is a devilishly sensitive subject to discuss. I'm glad it's over. Well, here's how!"

Emilio raised his glass in salute. He took a long swallow and then said, "I guess now it's all right if you let me know who the patient is?"

"Yes, of course. It's ridiculous to assume you wouldn't find out anyway." He smiled. "And I don't believe there's any need to remind you of your professional vows?" Emilio lowered his head. "Laura Bartlett," Dr Stone said. "Know her? Her father is president of the County National."

"Laura Bartlett?" Emilio repeated slowly.

"You may have seen her around. Dark. Slim. Rather delicate. Friend of the Lambertson girl and Clara Taylor." Emilio shook his head. "It's better that way," Dr Stone said. "In her present state it would add to her uneasiness. You know how these things are. Terrific emotional unbalance. After it's all over just as if nothing had ever happened. Far as I could gather, she's been going around with this chap about three or four months. Met him down in the city. One of those whirlwind romances, you know. Then suddenly you wake up. Well, there it is and there she is. We've got to do what we can."

"Tomorrow morning around ten," Emilio said. "I'll be all ready. You'll send a nurse along."

"Fine. Splendid. She'll be over at ten sharp. Another scotch or cognac?"

"Thanks. I've got to be going now. A few things I have to do." He smiled. "If there's any change in the plans, just phone me. In any case, I'll call you this evening." At the door he paused. He looked up at Dr Stone and said in an offhand way, "Incidentally—over at your club! I expect my name'll be coming up for membership at the next meeting. If you could say a word, I'd certainly appreciate it."

"How? Why, yes—yes, of course," Dr Stone said after a slight hesitation. "I wasn't following for the moment. Anything, old chap. I'll do what I can," shaking Emilio's hand vigorously. He followed along through the hall to the front entrance and waited while the nurse handed Emilio his hat and coat. He said good-by again, smiling—confident.

As Emilio got into his car and headed away through the drive he laughed to himself. He couldn't help it. His mood was expressed in the way he gripped the steering wheel and stepped down on the accelerator, and his laughter grew out of a floating feeling of excitement.

12

WITH the Italians on Wop-Roost hunting was serious business, matter-of-fact, like work, an air of importance attached to it. But the card games on Sunday afternoons were something else. Relaxation, taking it easy after the toil and struggle of the week. When Marco suggested that they get together for an hour or two and start cleaning up all the loose junk lying around they looked at him as if he was mad—the beginning of suspicion that this stranger might become annoying with his constant desire to accomplish things. "Tomorrow," Beppo argued. "Today, Sunday, we play the poke. Is Vincenzo here last game he clip me ten cents. Now I get the revenge. Plenty time make the cleanup. Is no a job easy to do like you say. Have to think lilla while. Hurry up, clean up like this, maybe I throw away something next months I need. No good be in such a hurry."

Marco laughed. With the exception of Nick all the Italians had gathered in Luca's shack waiting for Luca's wife to clear the table so the game could get under way. Tony was on the floor, crouched on his hands and knees, giving one of the kids a horseback ride. Pretty soon Dina would take the kids and go off to a meeting of the women in one of the other shacks where they rolled tremendous sheets of dough for Italian noodles and rehashed the gossip of the village snatched up during the hour at church. "All right," Marco said. "Today is the poker game. But tomorrow, who has not a job to do will spend the time to make his place look a little bit decent."

"Fine!" Luca joked, pounding his stomach. "I am too much full now to work. But tomorrow I make the place shine like polish. Even I wash myself—maybe. Hey, Dina, you hear? No more this wop-style house. Everything I want spick like span. Salamangonia, pretty soon I make her talk with the lips close, just like Giustina." He roared with laughter, slapping Marco on the back while Dina scowled.

"Imbecille!" she said, shaking the dishrag in his face. Then to Marco, "You ask him from which side this family come the best refine. You ask. Even my mamma say I marry him is just like to marry the pig. Is become just like the pig all right." She puffed out her cheeks and made a grunting sound.

Giuseppe spilled a jar of dried kidney beans on the table

and began to count them into little piles of so many for a cent. He wanted to know if Marco was going to play. "I am going with Nick," Marco said. "We will try to get some work pruning trees. With his leg bad I can help him."

"You forget the work for now," Tony said, grabbing his arm. "You play. Here, I lend you myself fifteen cents," taking a greasy change purse from his pocket. Immediately Giuseppe slapped a quarter down on the table. "Put away you money, Tony! Is here plenty for Marco if he want. Is the money you worry, Marco?"

"It is the money all right," Marco laughed. "But not to play cards. The money to know how I will live next week." He raised his hand in salutation, waving the Italians to their game. "I will be back after. Good luck."

Outside Marco turned up the road to Giuseppe's house. He stopped for a moment, looking over the rooftops of the village below, to the weather-stained shingles of the Gardella home. He leaned against a tree and rolled a cigarette. He lit the cigarette, flicked the match into the air and remained for some time without moving. Then the sound of a footstep wakened him from his revery. It was Angela. She smiled and came close, following his gaze over the scene below. "What are you doing?" she asked, her voice coming from far away as if it had nothing to do with what she was thinking.

Marco blew the ash from his cigarette. "I was looking down there," he said quietly. Then he added in a lighter vein, "But you! Home on the afternoon of Sunday? It is very strange."

"Oh, I'm not staying home," Angela replied. "I'm going dancing. I'm going out with some boys from the village."

Marco cocked his head to one side. Angela said quickly, "I have lots of boy friends. I don't have to depend on any particular one."

"Of that I am sure."

A silence followed. It became strained. "I know what you're thinking," broke suddenly from Angela. "You're thinking about me and Doctor Gardella. You wonder why I'm not going out with him today."

"What you do is not my business," Marco said with amusement.

"Well, I'm not a fool. I'm not a dishrag. He thinks I don't know he has one of those rich girls in town; that's why he doesn't want me along. Well—well, he can go to hell!" She almost shouted the final sentence, as if she had to impress her determination upon the whole colony. She turned and started to walk away down the road. "Wait a minute!" Marco called. But she continued on, her head held high and looking straight ahead.

Nick came slowly over from the house dressed in his coat with the crinkly fur collar and his black fedora hat which set him apart from the other Italians. He glanced somewhat puzzled at Marco and at the swaying movement of Angela's body as she moved further from sight. "Whatsamatter now?" he asked.

"Nothing," Marco shrugged. "The complications of love. She had some kind of a fight with Doctor Emilio and now she is going out with somebody else just to show him she does not care. The young girl! What can you do for a thing like that? You just listen and keep quiet, that is all."

"And Giuseppe tell me I got the eyes bad," Nick said. "Is him blind like a stone. You think anything good come with Angelina from that salamambitch doctor? You think fifty times first. You know yourself what kind fellow he is. Here, the leg! He say he come back to look if everything all right. You see him?" He brushed his hand under his chin. "You see you grandmother first!"

Marco didn't answer. "For Angelina I am just the oncle," Nick continued. "Me, is to keep my face close. Giuseppe the papa. Okay. Okay. I make the shut-up." He slid his hand into Marco's arm. "But comes something bad, then you see how I talk. You see all right."

Marco hurried to change the subject. "Now is the worry to find some work. How the leg feels? You think you can walk?"

Nick stamped his foot on the ground. The leg was fine. Just a little pain when he bent the knee too much. They proceeded slowly down the hill to the village, Marco shortening his stride to make it easier for Nick. "Is plenty work we can get," Nick said enthusiastically. "Plenty rich place around here where they need somebody take care the fruit trees. Me, I get mad when the people no onderstand what I talk. But you, you speak fine—like professore. So, you make the salesman and I be the specialist. On the job we work to-gether. Is fine combination."

As they approached the village they saw Federico's Packard coming in their direction and they stepped aside, waiting for it to pass. The huge vehicle seemed to be rolling along driverless, and then they caught a glimpse of Elena, low, smiling, behind the wheel. She brought the car to a halt right beside them. "Hello," she called, leaning out of the window. "Where you going?"

Marco tipped his cap in greeting. Nick poked his fingers at his mouth and laughed. "We take a walk to find some work to buy the macaroni. You know somebody need couple foist-class men?"

"Maybe," Elena said. "Come on, get in."

They looked at each other and got into the car, Marco up front with Elena and Nick in back, comfortable against the soft cushions with his legs stretched out and his hands deep into his pockets. "Ho, ho, Elena!" he said with childish de-light. "Sometime you let me take one pitch myself like this. I send home to the wife and the kids. They think I become millionario. Instead castor oil, Mussolini he send me gold invitation come back and bring the money."

They all laughed. As Elena drove on again she explained, "We have some people very much interested in taking over that Smith farm up here. Only they want it in decent shape. If you could give me a figure on cleaning the orchards and the vineyard, I might be able to give you the work."

"Sure we give you estimate," Nick said quickly. "By the

day? Or we make contract for the whole job? Any way you want." Then his voice fell a little. "So you sell the place?"

"I think so," Elena answered. She could feel Marco watching her. Keeping her eyes on the road ahead, she added, "Do you know the farm we are talking about? It's the one just across from the swamp."

"I know. I know all about it. Three years the land is idle. Three years the land going to waste. It is shame on the people who own such a farm."

"It isn't our fault we have the place on our hands," Elena said. "Besides, we're not in the farming business."

"Business!" Marco repeated. "Farming is not a business. It is like a profession. A man does not kill himself on the soil because he thinks he is going to get rich. It is because he loves the ground and from the ground comes everything that will keep him alive and happy. Ah, the good farmers I have seen! You should know them too." He grinned, nodding his head at some recollection. "For them the land is like a woman. They get mad. They curse. They holler all the names up in the sky to swallow the farm. But when there is nobody to look they get down on their knees and kiss it. That is the real farmer. That is the love of the ground. Business. Poogh! Business is for the man in the grocery store who knows how to sell the spaghetti and the potatoes in the tin cans. Tomorrow he will do something else and the day after something else again. And when he grows old he begins to shrink and he cries in that little voice, 'What I have got from this life?' Not the farmer who lives with his land. At almost one hundred I have seen him again and again, the eyes alive, happy—drink the wine, eat the good food, laugh, joke. What has he got to be afraid? Die? He will laugh. Out the window he will point to the chestnut tree that he planted when he was a little boy. He will show you the field and his children there with the children of his children, still working the same ground from before anybody can remember. He is there. Every-place he looks he can see himself. He has nothing to shout and nothing to cry. And for him to die is easy like to close his eyes and fall asleep."

Now they were going down the other side of Wop-Roost, through the valley where the ice-coated stream glistened in the sun. Elena swung the car into a narrow lane off the road to the right. Tall dry weeds swished against the fenders, cracked and fell low beneath the passing wheels. The faded white farmhouse approached closer and the barn rose to their eyes with its sagging roof and shingles that the wind had torn away. Elena stopped the car and they got out—silent, blinking somewhat foolishly at the desolate hillside which sloped gradually upward to the orchards and the vineyard. It was as if each of them had known this place, could picture it in his mind and was suddenly shocked by its echoing emptiness.

Nick coughed. He became very businesslike, brought out a stub of pencil and a little notebook. "Well," he said. "First, before anything, I make the check up on watch you got here. Look to me like a job, better we take by the day or we find we get stuck. You 'scuse, please. I go see the condition the trees and count how many be prune, how many chop down." He started off across the field with his gimpy stride, pencil and notebook in hand, studying the skeleton trees on the side of the hill and shaking his head.

Elena unlocked the door of the farmhouse. She peered inside, then turned and watched Marco pull at a tangle of grass to uncover a carefully laid stone walk leading from where the car stood to the entrance. "Do you suppose anybody could ever make a living out of a place like this?" she asked.

Marco seemed surprised at the question. Then, as though remembering something, a trace of scorn showed on his lips. "Do you think that the man who first put down the stones here had trouble to keep himself alive and his family? Do you think that his friend who was in business in the village had a better life than him?"

"I don't know," Elena said. "I only know that his son couldn't do anything with the farm. It went slowly to ruin. The father owned the place free and clear. The son had to borrow money and he lost the money and everything else besides." She said this with a challenge in her voice.

"And why did this happen? There must be a reason. So long as ground will produce there is always a market for the man who works it. People must eat. They must depend on the farmer."

"Well, here you have proof that he couldn't make a go of it."

"This is only the proof the man was not a farmer. Give me a piece of land like this and three or four men from up on the hill and I will show you if we can keep it. Silly to talk the way you talk. It is like to say because one farmer could not keep himself alive, you will take all the rest of the farmers and make them into something else. And for vegetables the public will eat pills. What a beautiful idea!"

"It wasn't vegetables," Elena laughed. "It was peaches. Farmers made a lot of money out of peaches in this section some fifteen years back. Only everyone else got the same idea. Peaches and nothing else. Young Smith along with the rest of them. Then the market was killed. Also a few severe winters which froze the blossoms. There you have the story."

"I know," Marco said. "Nick told me everything. Now Mister Smith has a job in the town for twenty-five, maybe thirty dollars every week. But the collar on his shirt is clean. He has lost the farm and he is glad because he is no more what they call—what they call"—Marco snapped his fingers and wrinkled his face in a painful effort—"hick. That is what I mean."

After a pause in which he allowed himself the pleasure of Elena's amusement Marco said, "Well, it is nice to talk. But it is not so nice to leave all the work for my partner." He looked at her, hating to go away, and then started slowly across the field to the orchard where the stubby figure of Nick moved in and out among the fruit trees in the distance.

"Wait a minute," Elena said.

Marco turned around. Elena stepped from the doorway and went forward to him. It was as if what she wanted to say hurt her in trying to come out. "I was only fooling about selling this farm," she said. "We have nobody who wants to buy it. I just was anxious to know. That is, my father and I have been talking the thing over and we were wondering if you and Nick and some of the other Italians would be interested in running it. It's nothing definite. Just an idea. A business proposition. From what you said this morning, I sort of felt——"

At first Marco didn't understand. The hesitancy of her speech and her confusion impressed him more than what she was actually saying. Then he realized with a shock which left him a little weak on his legs. "You are fooling. You are fooling with me," he said in a voice suffocated and angry.

"Why should I fool you? I'm not promising anything. You seem to have such confidence in these people and your own ability as a farmer. It might be a fair risk to let you have the place for a couple of years on a sort of share basis. Why not? We don't stand to lose anything much."

"But your mother? Your brother?" Marco said. "They will never say yes to anything like this."

"If it concerns business and we have nothing to do with actually working the farm? If they can see a possibility to turn loss into profit?"

Marco turned his head away. He tried to smile. But it was

only a half smile, undecided. "This is something I want to do myself," Elena said, "for my own satisfaction. I mean this farm. The things I've heard you say which seem so much like my own thoughts—thoughts I never could quite grasp before. That's why I say this would be something for myself, something I could stand up to against them and they'd have to give in because I feel it strongly, as they feel strongly about money and ambition and getting somewhere in the way most people consider." Her shoulders sagged helplessly. "I don't know exactly what I mean. It was all clear to me this morning after I left you and now I'm all in a muddle again. But if you really believe you and the Italians up on the hill could do something with this place, I think I could get it for you, no matter how my mother and brother feel about it. That's what I mean."

Elena paused, confused, embarrassed at the stream of words which had poured from her. Marco was silent. When he spoke he kept his head lowered, talking to the earth, not trusting himself to address her directly. "You know what kind of a man I am. You see how I have come here off the road. I am a bum. Your brother thinks this, and your mother too. For them my promise is nothing. Maybe for you, too, and your father. But for the Italians up there I can promise that if you let them work this farm you will never be sorry and never have to be ashamed. Every penny you give to help them you will get back. And as long as there are hands to work, the promise will never be broken. I swear this to you."

There came another strained interval of silence. Then Elena said, "Well, I guess that's all there is for now. Do you want me to say anything to Nick, or will you tell him yourself?"

"I will tell him," Marco said. "If you want I will come with Nick to see your father. Nick knows about the trees and the cultivation of the vines. The rest I know myself. We will convince your father. Maybe we can convince your mother too. And if you say something yourself, even your brother will not fight too hard. But it must be soon! The trees have to be pruned and the vines cleaned. There is plenty of work before the spring. In another month it will be too late." His voice began to falter. "I—I——"

"That's all right," Elena laughed. "I'll leave you now. I've got to get back. In a day or two I think I can let you know definitely. Meantime you can plan exactly what you want to do and how you want to go about it, so if I should ask you to the house, you will know exactly what to say."

She walked slowly to the car. Marco followed and as she started the motor he leaned through the window and held out his hand. Elena took it. She smiled and in another moment the limousine was away down the lane. Marco watched it turn into the road, cross the little plank bridge over the stream and head up the hill to Wop-Roost. It seemed to him, when the car was almost out of sight, he saw Elena wave and he raised his hand to wave back.

Nick had seen the car go away and began to shout excitedly from the orchard. Marco beckoned to him. Then he walked over to the door of the farmhouse and looked inside. He noticed the key still in the lock and removed it. When Nick came up to him he was standing quietly with the key in the palm of his hand, staring at it.

"Whatsamatter that girl?" Nick puffed. "First she take us here, then she run away! Now with the leg I gotta walk again over the top that goddamn hill. She crazy just like everybody else in that house." He put his hand to his head. "Madonna! You go up there and look youself those trees. Is no possible give estimate that kind work. Maybe take three time what we think. I forget was in such bad shape. But what the hell we care? We take by the day. When we finish, we finish. The people got the money to buy this place they pay. Is probabla people from the city want country place just for the show." He stopped talking suddenly and moved close to Marco. His eyes rested on the key and traveled upward. What he saw in Marco's face made him forget about the key and his annoyance at having to walk back with his bad leg. "Marco," he whispered. "Marco. Why you look like this? Something happen?"

Marco nodded. He put his arm around Nick's shoulder and managed to grin a little. But it was another minute before he could talk.

13

THE FIRST THING Emilio did when he returned home was to grab up his mother and whirl her around in his arm, leaving her breathless, holding her heart and giggling. "Well, I did it," he said, throwing his hat on the living-room sofa. He even slapped his father on the back. "I didn't have to go to them. They came to me. I knew it. I knew it all the time." Then to his mother, "Oh, before I forget! Take out my tuxedo tomorrow and give it a pressing. I'll need it Tuesday night. I'm going down to the city with Hazel and a few friends on a theater party I'm throwing. Boy, oh, boy! Now with Stone to back me up on the professional side and that dope Joe Simons and Hazel's father, I'm in! Right smack where I want to be. God, it sounds too good to be true." He hugged Giustina again and smiled broadly to Elena as she edged into the room. "I'll get an office in town. A nurse. A nice flashy car—Cadillac maybe. Stop in at the club every day for lunch or a drink and chew the fat with the big muckety-mucks."

"And from where gonna come all the money for this?" Federico inquired.

"Keep shut up!" Giustina said out of her excitement. "Give him chance to finish talk. What happen, Emilio? What happen with the big doctor?"

"What happened?" Emilio repeated with pretense at amazement. "What do you think? Very simple. Doctor Stone needs me to take care of a special case for him. Something very difficult he feels I can handle better than anybody else." He leaned close to his mother and whispered, "Five hundred dollars! Five hundred smackers!"

Federico whistled. "Five hundred dollar! Must be contract you get to take care somebody for one years."

"Don't be silly. What do you think these people are, the wops up on the hill? Altogether I may be busy about a half a day. That's the way to be a doctor! That's what I've been trying to make you understand. A couple of hours, half a grand. Now you see why I wanted to cultivate Doctor Stone and that crowd. Now you can holler like a miser about the couple of dollars you used to hand me."

"Was no me," Giustina hurried to say. "You know alla time I say if the money is for to help you you have watch you want. You know that. Was him, the stupid with the fat face and the mustache."

Now as Giustina held on to Emilio's arm and scowled at

her husband Elena interfered. "Let's not get excited. Just take it easy." She turned to Emilio. "Doctor Stone may be well off. But why should he turn a case over to you when he could pocket the fee himself? Don't tell me he's that altruistic."

Emilio looked at the ceiling. He tapped his foot on the floor. "Because I happen to be the one most qualified to handle the case! Isn't that enough? He saw what I could do at the hospital. What's five hundred to Stone? The prestige in simply being able to advise is worth more to him than that. Why, as physician his cut alone is probably more than what I'll get. Don't be a damn fool all your life, will you?"

"Elena!" Giustina said sternly.

"All right," Elena said. "I'm not trying to pry into your affairs. I was just trying to understand, that's all. But tell me this: Is it an operation?"

"Of course. An extremely delicate one too. Anything else you'd like to know? I'll answer anything." He said this with an air of boredom.

"I know that. You'll answer anything in your own way. You'll get very technical too," Elena said weakly. "And I suppose you're going to perform this operation at the hospital?"

"No. Right here in my own place. One of those cases where the patient has a deadly fear of hospitals and institutions of any kind. It can't be helped. Oh, nuts! Questions! Questions! I don't know why the hell I bother to come

home at all. What am I now, a kid, I have to explain everything, give reasons for every move I make? I'm fed up with
the whole goddamn business."

Giustina coaxed. She wheedled him into keeping calm.
After all, Elena was only interested in his welfare, as they
all were. Federico remained silent. He stood near the wall
fooling with the indicator of the new automatic thermostat
which governed the oil burner. He watched Elena, noting
the immobility of her expression, the dulled pain which
seemed to emanate from behind her blank stare. Giustina
continued to ingratiate herself to Emilio. "Everything from
lunch I have save for you in the icebox. You hongry? Five
minutes everything be ready. Dio mio, you go away all day!
You no telephone. But you mamma she think of you. Now
take off the coat. We sit down. You eat and you tell me
again from the start what the big doctor he tell you and
what you tell him and what you say to the girl. So tomorrow you make the operate? Day after you go to the teatro,
dress swell with the girl on the arm like this, like I see the
rich people in the paper. Five Hundred dollar! You make
one operate every week and you have the money to burn.
And they tell me I was no so smart make you doctor. They
tell me. Ha, ha. Come on, take off the coat."

"I can't," Emilio said. "Really, I'm not hungry. I had a
good lunch and tea just a little while ago. I only stopped
in to tell you the news and to tell you not to forget to press
my tuxedo."

"I no forget. You no have to worry for that."

"Why don't you go out to the movies tonight? Hey, sappy!" to Elena, "why don't you take Mamma and the old man to town? There's a good picture there, I understand." Then to Giustina again, "No, I couldn't eat a thing. I mean it. I got to go now. See you all in the morning."

Emilio picked up his hat. He kissed his mother lightly on the cheek to make her feel good. Giustina followed him to the door, still holding his arm. She watched him go down the steps and closed the door quickly to prevent the house from cooling. She wrapped her shawl tight about her shoulders and rocked her head proudly. Then she sighed heavily, as though there was something sad in this moment which culminated a lifelong ambition for herself and her son.

"You'd better get dressed," Elena said, "if you want to go to the movies. Are you coming along?" she asked her father.

Federico flung a hand in the air. "The moon-pitch! Alla time the same thing. The love. The talk so fast I no onder-stand from nothing. I stay here by myself. I have peace, quiet for change. Is the best thing for me."

"We leave him home," Giustina said. "He no care to see how nice people live—what is the life someplace else. And every five minuts he gotta get up to go in the back." She hurried to change her house dress.

Elena went to the mirrored door of the closet in the hall and began slowly to powder her face. She put on her hat. Federico came over and helped her with her coat. He stood watching as she pulled on her gloves and studied herself in the mirror. "Elena," Federico said softly.

"Yes."

Federico rubbed his chin. "Why you ask Emilio so many question? You have the suspish for him? You think maybe somebody take him for fool—make him do something wrong?"

"What could anyone make him do he didn't want to do himself?"

"What I know what? Is the way you talk make me think maybe was something."

"No," Elena said. "It's nothing. We can't run his life for him. Maybe he knows what he's doing. I hope so."

Federico was more puzzled than ever. He looked at his daughter with the same mingled feeling of annoyance and exasperation he usually reserved for Emilio. He was about to press her further but he heard his wife coming down the stairs. "All right," he said. "You go with you mamma the moon-pitch now. Tomorrow we talk. Smell something I no like here."

In the drugstore Emilio gave an account of himself to the druggist in much the same manner he had given it to his family, only putting most of the emphasis on the romantic portion of the afternoon. After leaving Dr Stone, he had phoned Hazel and picked her up at her house. "Jesus, when I told old lady Lambertson I'd just come from a consultation with Stone you should have seen the change in her attitude. She wasn't so damn snooty any more. Like I said. It's tough to get in, but once you're in you're in for good. Anyway, I took Hazel for a drive and we stopped for tea in one of these roadhouses along the way. Ah, there's no getting away from it—when a girl's got class, when you feel there's something there, you don't mind making a sap of yourself. Sometimes I can be the most romantic dope in the world. I tell you I've fallen for her, hook, line and sinker. Just wait awhile. Just wait till I get going. I'll grab her off over the heads of all those suckers she got smelling around now—the ones the old lady thinks are such marvelous possibilities."

"What about that other guy?" the druggist asked. "The guy you met at the club. You see him?"

"Oh, you mean the horse's ass?" Emilio laughed. "I gave him a buzz too. We're all fixed up for a theater party Tuesday night. Him and his girl and me and Hazel. Don't worry, I don't miss a trick." He dug his hands into his pockets and grimaced. "Hell, here I was all worked up and she has to go someplace tonight with her mother. But she promised to call me when she got home. A last good night before bedtime. I'm going completely nuts on this romance stuff. Oh, Christ! Close up the shop. It's seven o'clock. You won't get any more customers. I'll buy you a couple of drinks someplace."

The druggist blinked in horror at the suggestion. "Don't even mention it. If I left the place the wife'd skin me alive. Just a little while ago we had a hell of a battle about me sneaking off so much. Here, you want a shot? I got some here."

Emilio shook his head. He paced back and forth across the floor, speaking in a low mumble as if to himself. "I ought to turn in early, get a good night's rest for tomorrow. But damn it, I'm all worked up. I need some excitement. Got to get the steam out of me somehow." He stopped suddenly and looked up at the druggist, a grin stretching across his face. "What about Angela? She been in since this morning?"

The druggist shook his head. "But just before dark Billy Dexter came in for a pack of cigarettes and I saw her outside in the car with the gang of the kids having one hell of a time."

"Trying to make me jealous," Emilio said scornfully. Then he snapped his fingers. "The Valley Rest! That's where she said they were going. I'll take a run over there and have some fun. See you in the morning."

"Wait a second," the druggist said. He seemed dubious. He leaned over the counter with his chin on his arm. "Now look, Emile. You got that kid in an awful state. Not that I give a damn—it's none of my business. But you ought to go easy now. Let her alone. The more you see her, the more difficult it'll be to get rid of her after. I'm telling you for your own good. What's the use of making the complications worse? You keep fooling around and something'll leak out sure and then you will be in a mess."

Emilio grew petulant. "You're getting like my old man

and my sister. What am I supposed to do, stay home and twiddle my thumbs?" His petulance took on a quality of smugness. "After all, it's a fifty-fifty proposition. She gets as much fun as I do. You think she's fool enough to open her mouth? Listen. Ten years from now when she's hooked up with some bohunk it'll give her something to look back on and remember." He paused with a smirk on his face.

"You know what you're doing," the druggist said. "I can't blame you much. I don't care what you say about all those dames in town with money and finishing-school background and all that. They got to go some to offer a guy what this girl has in honest-to-God sex appeal. Why, I watch Angela sometimes and I got to get around in back of the counter. I don't know exactly what the hell it is, but it's something. Man!"

"It's the same with me," Emilio said. "If I'm lying in bed and I start thinking about women, right away I've got Angela there before my mind. I'll be damned. Every time. It's just like I can't imagine anybody else. Drives me nuts sometimes." He moved toward the door, laughing. "And you pulling the moralist stuff while she's out there wasting her talents on a bunch of kids. The hell with you, Jack!"

The druggist laughed. He continued to watch through the glass door as Emilio disappeared into the night. Then he gazed about the emptiness of the store and heard the loud beats of the electric clock on the wall in front of him. He opened the drawer for his bottle of whisky, barely moistened his tongue and put the bottle away, somewhat disgusted. He sighed and lowered his head on his arms, staring vacantly at a huge cockroach as it scurried across the floor and up one of the legs of the stove to sizzle and fall lifeless.

Federico alone. The house warm and comfortable and outside the cold, clear night and the limitless sky and stars and here a man shut away by himself, growing old and dying by himself—a man alone. There was the wine gallon sitting on the floor from dinner and the empty rocking chair with the hollow in the pillow from years of sitting and rocking and falling asleep. There were the Sunday papers where he had left them with all the headlines he hadn't read or couldn't understand, and the pictures he did understand but which meant nothing to him unless he could talk about them and make opinions and in this way establish the connection between himself and what he saw. There was the money in his pocket which he jingled as a child jingles washers, knowing their worthlessness and yet clinging stubbornly to the belief that they may not be washers but the wherewithal to purchase what he pleases and the possession alone to raise him above the level of others.

He went to the kitchen, to the icebox and cut a thick slice of salami, parading through the house from one room to the next, perfectly free to do as he pleased. He poured a full glass of wine and swallowed it in one gulp and filled the glass again, passing his hand over his mustache and curling the hairs into his mouth to suck the beady drops of wine lingering there. He smiled to himself and ran his fingers lightly over the smooth surface of the table. Then he searched far into a drawer of the buffet for an old deck of cards and played a game by himself, setting a handful of change at his side and making stakes which he collected and paid to himself. After a few hands he grew tired and wandered about the house again, humming and flicking his finger against his lip in order to produce unusual sound effects. He rummaged behind all the old clothes hanging in the hallway closet and pulled out a double-barrel shotgun with fistulas of rust beginning to eat through the metal. He clicked his tongue and tried to rub the rust away with his palm. For a time he stood in the living room and aimed the gun at different objects, emphasizing the click of the trigger on the empty chamber with a loud Bam-m-m! from his throat.

A short while later he put on his coat and hat and walked up the darkened street to the drugstore. "Allo! Allo!" he greeted the druggist. "You have Italiano cigar for me?" The druggist handed him a cardboard box filled with long, stringy cigars, tapering at both ends and resembling barnacled dog turds. He selected one, removed the band in the colors of the Italian flag and cut the cigar in half with his pocketknife, sticking one of the ends into his mouth. "Is good smoke this kind cigar sometimes," he said in a friendly tone.

"Smoke them myself every now and then," the druggist

said. But he was sleepy and not inclined to conversation. Federico tried to think of something else to say. It was difficult. "Emilio. He was here tonight?"

"He was here but he left some time ago. He was going someplace."

Federico nodded. He puffed on the Italian cigar and blew a deep blue cloud of smoke to the ceiling. "Well, good night," he said. And the druggist answered, "Good night."

Now Federico was outside again with the red glow of the cigar before his face, staring at the illuminated sign in front of his son's house and the building dark and empty behind it. He shrugged his shoulders and looked up into the sky, at a slice of moon just beginning to peer over the hill of Wop-Roost. His eyes fell lower, to the points of light through the trees which marked the shacks. He took a deep breath and started slowly along the incline in the direction of the lights.

Dogs came running as he approached near, barking, growling, but standing their distance like cowards. Through the window of Luca's shack he could see the Italians seated at their card game, glasses full, laughing and shouting as they slammed their cards down on the table. Beppo leaned over, cupping his hands to his eyes to see what was exciting the dogs, and drew away again with an indifferent motion. Federico hesitated for some time and then continued on to Giuseppe's house, past the shack belonging to Tony where the women and children bobbed up and down in a puppet show of happy faces. In Giu-

seppe's house, beneath the glare of the electric bulb hanging from the ceiling, he saw Marco and Nick, their shirts
open at the collar and kneeling over the table with a piece
of wrapping paper spread out before them, Marco pointing
with a pencil while Nick stood to one side shaking his head
and talking excitedly with his hands. He walked on a little
further, with Giuseppe's dog trailing and sniffing at his
heels, over the rise of the hill and back again slowly. Now
Nick had the pencil and Marco stood in the middle of the
room talking with his arms spread in a sweeping gesture
which seemed to gather the whole world to himself. He
tried to follow the movement of Marco's lips, fascinated,
unable to understand anything. But from the expression on
Marco's face he knew it was something wonderful and he
felt pained to be unable to join them. There was a strange-
ness between him on the outside and the men in there
built from the years of living down below and he couldn't
overcome it. In a little while he started down the hill again
to the village, now conscious of a sudden uneasiness that
someone might come out and see him.

14

AS FEDERICO was about to enter the house he noticed that the illuminated sign across the street had been switched off, though apparently Emilio was not at home. Then he caught a faint glimmer of light coming from the edge of one of the windows, and he saw that all the dark shades were drawn to their full length. This puzzled him. Ordinarily he would have put the matter out of his mind rather than risk the unpleasantness of sticking his nose into Emilio's private affairs. But tonight it was different.

He crossed over to the other side of the street, stepped quietly along the narrow walk and up the steps to the porch. He put his ear to the door and listened. No sound came to him from within and he became more at ease. He tried the doorknob lightly. The door was locked. He smiled and prepared to rattle the doorknob vigorously, in the usual manner of announcing himself. Just then he heard a low, prolonged giggle from the throat of a girl, and Emilio's hushed voice saying something he couldn't catch. The voices came from far inside. It was impossible for him to hear plainly.

On tiptoe he went down the steps again and stole around the side of the house, standing beneath the windows of the bedroom. It seemed like an eternity before he heard anything again, and then, as before, the rollicking giggle. This time, however, he had no difficulty hearing Emilio as he said, "Keep quiet, Angela, for God's sake! You'll wake the whole neighborhood." Federico froze against the house.

"What do you care?" Angela said. "There's nobody home. You said they went to the movies."

"I know, but they'll be back. Why do you think I parked the car way down the street?"

"And even if they did find me here?" Now her voice was peculiar and floating, as if she were a little drunk. "Even if they did? They'll find out anyway sometime." Then in a lighter tone, "What you told me in the car? Tell me that again. Come in here beside me and tell me that again."

"All right. All right. Drink this first. It'll straighten you up. You'll have to get out of here by ten anyway. I got to get up early."

"I don't want anything. I'm feeling fine. I love it and it's all your fault." Next Federico heard the crashing of a glass on the floor and the shrill laughter all over again and Emilio saying, "You crazy little wop! You're insane." And softer, "But you're marvelous. Wonderful. I'm crazy about you."

Federico stumbled away in the darkness to his own house. He snapped on the light button in the hallway and removed his coat, staring at the haunted pallor of his face in the mirror. He went into the living room and fell down on the couch, brushing his hat aside and running his hands through his hair. "Dio mio!" he said with a gasp.

They were in the consultation room, Emilio clad in dressing gown and slippers, pacing back and forth nervously, while Angela sat calmly on the operating table, her legs dangling, and twirling her hat on the tip of her finger. She was smiling with obstinate coquettishness as she tossed her head to throw a silky curl of dark brown hair from her eyes. "I meant it," Emilio was saying. "It's time for you to go now, Angela. I have a tough day ahead of me tomorrow. You know what it means. I've got to get all the sleep I can."

"Oh, it's early," Angela said with a wide gesture. "You can sleep late. It's only ten o'clock. The middle of the day practically."

Emilio glanced at his wrist watch. "Jesus Christ, will you go? I swear I'll take you out someplace tomorrow night. We'll celebrate. I promise." He took hold of her arm and tried to urge her to her feet. Angela held on to the edge of the operating table, closed her eyes and shook her head. Then she laughed. "I won't. You can't make me. Give me a kiss."

"I'll give you a crack in the mouth in a minute. I'm getting sore now."

"Why don't we get married?" Angela said suddenly. "Then I wouldn't have to go home. We could be together all the time—like tonight."

Emilio didn't answer. Angela said, "You don't want to marry me?"

"What would I use for money?" Emilio said in exasperation. "Don't even think about anything like that now. Wait until I don't have to depend on my family any more, then we'll talk about it."

"But you just told me that from now on you'd be making plenty. You just said you're getting five hundred dollars for one operation tomorrow. You mean you don't want to marry me. That's it. You mean——"

"Oh nuts!" Emilio slammed his fist down on the top of the table. "That business again! For the last time, will you go home or do I have to throw you out? I hate to be tough but you're forcing me to it."

"And you forced me into other things too. I won't go," Angela said fiercely.

Emilio took a step forward and then the telephone rang. It was as if someone had suddenly struck him a terrific blow. He straightened and his face became green. "What's the matter?" Angela said. "Go ahead, answer it."

The first ring died away and was immediately followed by another. Emilio didn't move. "There won't be anybody there if you don't pick up the receiver soon," Angela added, twirling her hat again.

"Are you going?"

"I told you I'm not going home," she cried.

Emilio eased into the chair at the desk and slowly lifted the receiver to his ear. "Hello," he said in a strange voice. There was a pause. The receiver against his ear brought the color back and the lobe appeared flaming for an instant until the flush of embarrassment altered his entire face. "Yes. Of course. Of course I'm alone. Strange? No. I was just dozing off in a chair reading. Still half asleep. What? You know I'm glad you called. Naturally. What's that? I'll call you in the morning sure. Pick you up Tuesday night around five. I'll reserve the tickets. Good night." He pressed his mouth closer and pretended to laugh. "I'm sorry. Good night, darling," almost in a whisper.

He didn't turn around right away but lowered the receiver slowly into place. When he did turn he said, "I told you to go home. You asked for it yourself. Now you got it."

Angela hadn't moved from the operating table, only her hat had fallen to the floor and her legs were still. "Go on," Emilio said. "Make a scene. Tell me I'm a louse. You know what you should do in a case like this. Well, get it over with. The sooner the better. What did you expect? Me to marry you? You know damn well you never believed that. Me, a wop! Marrying a wop! I could commit suicide as far as my profession goes. Talk! Talk! Say something." He bent close, angry, flinging the words at her.

Angela raised her head. The brilliant hue of her lipstick seemed like the dazzle of ruby on alabaster. She swelled her breast and spit full into Emilio's face. Then she leaped from the table and flung herself at him, clawing and kicking, driving him back across the consultation room to the desk. Emilio grabbed her wrists and held her off. "You sonofa-bitch," she cried and continued to kick at his shins. She spit at him again. Emilio let go of one of her wrists and struck her with the side of his fist. She went reeling backward and sank to the floor. She got up on her knees, shaking her head.

Now Emilio yanked her to her feet, pushed her hat under her arm and pulled her to the front door. He opened the door, saw the lights across the street and shut it quickly, yanking her through the house again to the rear entrance. "Now get the hell home!" he said in a stifled breath and slammed the door shut.

For a moment Angela remained motionless, bewildered in the sudden night about her. Then she staggered forward and stumbled, tearing her stockings, scraping her hands and knees on the sharp gravel outside the house. She got up and started to run, and the movement of running brought hot tears and gulping sobs. She continued to run all the way home, tripping again, bruising herself more until she reached the top of the hill. Then, breathless, exhausted, the cold air in her face, she came to her senses.

As she passed the shacks and approached her own house she saw the door open and sprang quickly from the road to the shelter of a tree. Marco came out followed by Nick, who snapped off the light. They went by, taking their time, Marco saying, "We will wait. We will not say anything until we are sure. It is too wonderful to make them believe and then the dream breaks." And Nick's monotonous, drumming voice: "Contract. We want the contract. We do nothing without first the contract." She waited until they had vanished amid the shouts and exclamations as they entered Luca's shack. Then she ran for the house, flinging herself upon the bed in a heap.

Just about a half-hour later Marco and Nick returned with Giuseppe. Giuseppe was in a high mood. He emptied his change purse on the table and began to count, separating the pennies from the nickels. "Boy, boy, boy! Today I catch everybody with the pants down. Thirty cents. Never before I make such a cleanup job. The poke take the brains, is why I am so good. What chance those dopey guys with Giuseppe in game where you use the intelligenza?"

He put the money away and then leaned over the table to study the square of wrapping paper on which Marco and Nick had been working. "What you call this?" he asked.

"It is nothing," Marco said, winking at Nick. "It is just a plan for a farm. The perfect farm. Someday maybe we will have a farm like that."

Giuseppe laughed. "And someday I be President the United States." However, his interest was caught. "Hmmmm! Here the fruit. Here the grape. Here the corn.

The tomato. The cabbage. The beans. Everything. Is pretty good arrange."

"Pretty good!" Nick cried. "Look who talk. The pick and shovel tell the engineer how is to be build the bridge. Pretty good? Is perfect. A number one."

Giuseppe shook his head. He addressed Marco. "Because he read maybe two book ten years back he think he experts on everything." Then to Nick, "What I was before I come here? Please, you tell me that. I was undertake, or I was farmer? Foolish, stupid! Sometimes when you talk before the people I think you have the whatsamatter upstairs."

Nick appeared a little embarrassed. He only grinned and didn't answer. Marco folded the plan, put it into his pocket and slapped Giuseppe on the shoulder. "Never mind, Nick. He does not mean anything. He is only joking with you."

"Joke. Joke. Is full the teoria and the loud mouth. Comes the real practice and the work, I show you I know just the same anybody about the farm. And I no go to school and I no learn from the book." He grabbed up the clock and began to wind it savagely.

Nick kicked off his shoes and proceeded to undress while Marco sat on the edge of the cot watching Giuseppe, amused at his injured pride. Now Giuseppe put the clock down on the table again. He continued to sulk. He started off to bed without saying good night, first stopping to peek into his daughter's room. He shut the door quickly. "Ah, for one time she come home early. Maybe tomorrow she get up to look for some work." His anger left him, making

way for concern. He looked at Marco. "Work," he repeated. "What I am gonna do myself tomorrow? I am
suppose to fill the dirt on top the tank, or Meesta Gardella
he get somebody else. After the deer maybe he tell me go
to hell if I show up there." He shook his head.

"I do not think he will give the work to anybody else,"
Marco said. "It was not your fault for the deer. It was me.
I think you can go down all right."

"I need the work," Giuseppe said. He clicked his tongue.
"Is only maybe lilla more than half day but I need very
bad. If he chase me I no can help. I go down just the same.
Dio, what tough, salamambitch life with all the worry for
this and for that." He remained for a moment deeply perplexed. Then he sighed and went off to bed.

In a little while Marco switched off the light and eased
into the cot which creaked and swayed beneath the weight
of his body. He lay on his back with his arms folded under
his head staring into the darkness, and slowly vague outlines formed before his eyes and he could make out the
rounded bulk of Nick lying on the couch across the room.
"Good night, Nick," he whispered.

"Good night, Marco," Nick said. And after a silence he
added, "Giuseppe get mad. I no mean for him get mad.
Make me feel bad. He do too much for me I say the things
like this to him. Tomorrow we tell him about the farm.
It make him feel good right way."

"Yes," Marco said. "Tomorrow maybe we tell everybody."

There was the quiet again, the heavy breathing of Nick as he fell asleep. Outside the wind was coming up and it moaned through the trees. Marco lay awake. In the darkness he smiled to himself. As he was falling asleep a strange sound came to him from somewhere within the house. He rose on his elbow and listened. At first it seemed like the stifled cry of some small animal, but when he heard it again he knew. He got up and stepped softly across the room, placing his ear against the door of Angela's room. After listening for a moment, he went back to the cot. He pulled the blanket over his head but he could still hear the low, repressed sobs which came through the darkness from the depths of Angela's pillow.

Elena and her mother came home rather late from the movies. They hurried up the rear steps and into the kitchen, Giustina wringing her hands. "Every light in the house open! Five minuts I leave and that man he do everything to kill us. We work to make the electric company rich. We save and he throw everything away. Santa Madre, when I marry him must be the devil wish me bad luck!"

She snapped off the switch in the kitchen and started through the hall to the living room. However, as she passed the dining room she stopped with a gasp. There was Federico in his armchair, dead drunk. His vest was open, his tie pulled to one side. His head had fallen upon his chest and his arms dangled over the sides of the armchair. In one hand he still clutched a glass from which the wine had spilled in a dark puddle over the rug. The wine gallon lay empty on its side at the other end of the room. Giustina clasped her hands together and let out a loud wail. She staggered into the room and fell into a chair at the table, the tears beginning to stream down her cheeks, the prolonged lament as she watched the helpless, sodden figure of her husband.

Elena shook Federico. She removed the glass from his grasp and shook him again. "Papa! Here! Wake up!" she said in alarm. Federico grumbled. He opened his eyes and squinted about the room. He closed them and opened them again. Then he managed to rise from the armchair, looking at his wife and at Elena in dumb bewilderment. He took a few steps forward, his legs sagging under him and the whole tremendous weight of his body settling to the floor. Elena grabbed him. "Help me!" to her mother. "Don't sit there like you were paralyzed. Help me get him upstairs to bed."

Together they managed to get Federico up on his feet and support him to the staircase. Here he jammed his fist against the wall and refused to budge any further, remaining like a boulder wedged in the narrow canyon leading up to the bedroom. He rolled his head and made a braying noise with his lips. He shook himself free from their hands and climbed the stairs alone, staggering from side to side, balancing precariously on the edge of each step. In the bedroom he flopped down on the bed with a groan. He allowed Elena to remove his shoes, but when Giustina came close to struggle with his vest he pushed her away and rolled over on his stomach.

"We get Emilio," Giustina moaned. "I go call him. Maybe poison. Maybe die. Whole gallon of wine he drink. Dio! Dio! Never before I see him like this. He try to kill himself." She went to the side of the bed again and bent over Federico, pleading, "Why you try to kill youself with the wine, Federico? Why you scare me like this?"

Elena urged her away out of the bedroom. She closed the door. "Leave him alone. Don't get Emilio. Don't get anybody. Just let him sleep it off."

"But is the doctor he need. In the house we have the doctor right here."

"He'll be all right in the morning," Elena said. "You come and sleep with me in my room."

Giustina brushed the hair from her face and wiped her eyes. She followed Elena meekly. As she undressed she kept whimpering. She had suddenly lost all her fire and strength and nothing remained but a shriveled and ineffectual old lady. This drunkenness on the part of Federico was something so far removed from her understanding that it produced the effect of a catastrophe. "Why he get drunk like this? Why?"

"How should I know?" Elena said. "But I imagine there are times when everybody feels like getting drunk. Just let him sleep it off."

15

AT THE USUAL HOUR Federico came down for breakfast. As he appeared in the kitchen Giustina and Emilio
stopped talking and looked at him as if he were some kind
of a curiosity. Only Elena turned her eyes away. But there
was nothing of embarrassment or guilt in Federico this
morning. He was just plain sullen and with a rotten headache in the bargain. He took his place opposite Emilio and
swallowed a cup of black coffee. With his shaggy head of
hair, his wild mustache and puffed cheeks he looked as if
he had been living in a cave. "You certainly got a skinful,"
Emilio laughed. "You're damn lucky you were able to get
up at all."

Federico didn't answer. He held up his cup for Elena
to pour some more coffee. "Nice picture he was," Giustina

said. "And the wine on the rug. Like the cat, I should put the nose there and beat with a stick."

"Well, I got a lot of work ahead of me this morning," Emilio said. He leaned over and tapped his father on the arm. "I'm telling you, a couple of more drunks like that and you'll just about cash in. Take my advice."

Federico raised his head and nodded. "We see who is the first one cash in. We see that."

"What are you driving at?"

"You know what I drive. Inside youself you know." He held his eyes on Emilio, his face grim, serious, the more arresting because of his unusual pallor. Elena and Giustina bent closer over the table.

"I don't know what you're talking about," Emilio said. "Because you feel like hell after slopping up a gallon of wine, I suppose it's my fault? Oh, why should I get myself in a stew? Here I get up early to prepare for an operation that means my whole career and I run into this kind of nonsense. Nuts!"

"Nuts," Federico repeated. "Pretty soon we see how you say nuts."

Emilio shrugged his shoulders. As he folded his napkin and prepared to get up there came a timid knock on the back door. He went over to the window and looked slantwise out to the stoop. He pulled back suddenly. "It's Giuseppe!"

"What he want here?" Giustina said. "What that fellow think, he gonna get work after the trooble he make?"

"Maybe Emilio know what Giuseppe want," Federico said.

"I don't know anything about it," Emilio said. "I'm going back to my office. I can't waste time here."

Elena got up to go to the door. "You sit down, Elena," Federico said. He turned to Emilio. "Open the door."

"What the Christ——"

"Open the door!" Federico shouted at the top of his voice. The veins stuck out on his forehead and his eyes looked about ready to pop from their sockets. Emilio hesitated. Then he went over and pulled the door open for Giuseppe to enter, stepping aside as the serious little man stood with his hunting cap in his hand, his small wrinkled face red with the cold, and trying to express himself. At the first word from Giuseppe's lips Emilio smiled.

"Scusate," Giuseppe said. "I think maybe—maybe you want I fill up the trench on top the tank before the dirt freeze too hard?" mixing the language with his hands.

"So, is now you come for the work!" Giustina cried. Federico reached out under the table and kicked her in the shin. "Aiee!" she gasped. Then Federico said to Giuseppe, "Is no me take charge the job today. Is Emilio. You want Giuseppe work, Emilio?"

Emilio turned color. "What have I—— I don't—— Sure, if he wants to work, let him work. What do I care?"

Federico waved Giuseppe out of the house. "In the garage the tools. You find everything there." Emilio waited until Giuseppe had shut the door and then he shouted,

"What are you trying to do, make me look like a goddamn fool in front of those people?"

"He make the whole family look like jackass," Giustina said.

Federico put his hands over his ears and closed his eyes. Elena took hold of her mother and Emilio and made them go out of the kitchen. "Leave him alone. Can't you see he's upset?"

"He's upset all right. Drinking like a pig and then acting like he was cracked."

"Is the wine," Giustina cried. "The wine eat up his brains."

Elena poured Federico another cup of coffee and sat down at his side. She drew his hand away from his ear and held it. "What's the matter? What's the trouble?" Federico rocked his head in a tired motion and remained silent.

Up on the hill the Italians, grumbling, but true to their word, began to clean up the ground around their shacks. It was cold and they worked fast. Marco selected a spot just off the side of the road where the junk could be easily dumped into a truck and they spread out, fan shape, running back and forth from the shacks. Slowly the pile grew. Tin cans, bedposts, bottles, oil drums, automobile tires and rims, battered headlights, fenders, the frames of baby carriages, busted wheels, shattered glass and garbage. After a while it became like a game, raising this mountain of accumulated trash. They laughed and joked as they emptied burlap sacks of rubbish and hurried to fill them again. In the excitement they threw away things they would never before have dreamed of discarding. But it was the mood. Junk! Junk! And suddenly everything became junk to be tossed on top of the pile.

Nick took care of the little cleaning up there was to do around Giuseppe's place while Marco gave a hand here and there. But he was quiet. His usual carefree manner was gone. And as his voice joined the common laughter it was a trifle forced. Even when Luca paused after every trip with the sack, his hands on his hips, surveying the result and saying, "Beautifool! Beautifool! I never think a couple tin cans make so much differenza," he only smiled. And when Nick nudged him because of the secret they had together which the others didn't know as yet he pretended to be thinking of something else.

During an argument over throwing away a wash boiler which had somehow gotten peppered with bird shot Marco slipped off by himself. He circled around to Giuseppe's house and entered quietly, remaining for some time with his hands in his pockets and staring at the door of Angela's room. He paced back and forth, rolled a cigarette, took a few puffs and threw the cigarette into the stove. He stood near the table looking out of the window and methodically thumped his fist on the table. Finally he went over to the door and knocked.

There was no answer. He waited a little while, his hand uncertain, and knocked again. Then he turned the knob and pushed the door open. Angela lay propped against the pillow, her eyes straight before her. She didn't move as Marco came into the room. He stood beside the bed, towering over her, fingering one of the buttons on his sweater. He noticed how her eyes were inflamed and the red welt on the side of her cheek. He noticed too, for the first time, the interior of the room, its simple walls of composition board and the magazine clippings of motion-picture actresses all around. "I thought maybe you were sick," he said.

Angela still looked away from him. Marco pulled up the chair on which she had flung her clothing and sat on the edge, folding his hands in his lap. "Last night I heard you. All night. I did not sleep. If you will tell me what is the trouble, maybe I can help you."

Angela turned her head to one side. There was the quivering of her lips and the floating liquid of her eyes. "I am not young like you," Marco said. "But I have known what it is to be in love. I know there are some things if you talk about them you feel much better. But if you keep them inside they become just like poison. And that is bad."

After a prolonged silence Marco got up. "I cannot make you talk if you do not want to. But it is Doctor Emilio? Tell me that." For answer Angela drew the pillow to her face. Marco remained looking at her for a moment and then went out of the room, closing the door after him.

Mechanically he reached for his tattered overcoat and put it on. Outside he paused, taking a deep breath of the cold wind as it rushed against him. Down below he could hear the Italians shouting, again in some kind of good-natured argument, and close to him the chickens cackling contentedly in the coop as they pecked away at the floor. He walked away from the house, avoiding the road, through the tangle of blackberry brush, further from Wop-Roost and the village. He walked with his head up in the air and with the blackberry thorns clinging to his coat, pulling past them like a man dazed, insensible to anything but a desire to keep moving.

Where the land sloped down into the valley he stopped, traced the line of the ridge opposite and the horizon, his gaze slanting downward to the abandoned farmhouse, the idle land and the pencil line of stream with the ice now leaden beneath the snow-puffed sky. From his pocket he drew the plan of the farm he had made with Nick and unfolded it. He looked at the square of wrapping paper for a moment and then ripped it apart, crumpling the pieces in his fists. Then he continued walking again down into the valley and along the road. At the wooden bridge over the stream he climbed upon the narrow railing and sat with his hands dangling between his knees, facing the barren expanse of marshland.

Federico had finally left the house and driven over to the millpond to help his men square off another section of ice which he wanted cut and drawn before night and the snow which seemed to hang so inevitably in the air. Elena sat wearily at the mahogany desk in the living room and tried to work on her accounts. Overhead she could hear her mother walking in and out of the bedrooms, making the beds and dusting. For a long while she remained at the desk, just picking at the blotter with a pen, unable to concentrate on the long column of figures at her elbow. She threw her hair forward in front of her face and stared at the ledger through a filmy blur, shaking the hair back into place again. She got up and went searching for her handbag, then stopped in the hallway in front of the mirror and powdered her nose. She stretched her arms over her head, yawned in disgust and returned to the work with a determined frown. Giustina came downstairs, glanced into the living room and went on with her housework.

Some twenty minutes to a half-hour later she appeared in the doorway, calling excitedly, "Elena! Look! Quick, I show you something." Elena sprang from the desk and rushed after her mother. Giustina pointed out of the dining-room window. "There! You see? You and you papa so smart with Emilio. Look now the kind people he have for customer. Look the fancy car. What you got to say now?"

Elena watched the cream-colored roadster that had come to a stop in front of Emilio's house and the girl at the wheel getting out. She was slenderly built and wearing an expensive fur coat, the collar of which she drew close to her face before going up the steps. Even her hosiery had that quality of luxury apparent in everything about her.

Now Emilio came out on the porch. He had on his white clinical jacket which buttoned to the throat and made him seem so important. He smiled, bowed slightly and stepped aside, holding the door open for the girl to enter.

Giustina turned back to her daughter, too excited to notice the dead helplessness there in her face. "And just before! On the bus, the nurse come! Lilla fat woman with lilla valise and short hair like man. Dio, grazie! Everything come true. Everything what I dream. Emilio big doctor. Nurse. Fine people in big automobile to see him for operate. Just like I see in front my brains alla time. So happy I feel. . . ." And her happiness was in the tear which she wiped away with her finger.

She bent close to the window again as Emilio ran down to the car, started the motor and swung the vehicle a half circle in their direction and shot through the driveway. Giustina rushed into the kitchen. "Why he bring the car over here? Why he no leave outside where the people see what kind rich society he work for now? Tch, tch. Is foolish what he do."

Emilio drove the roadster into the garage and hurried back along the drive, saluting the men working in the icehouse. When he saw his mother stick her head out of the door he ran over to her, paying no attention to Giuseppe, who paused with the shovel in his hand to offer a friendly smile. Giustina pulled him into the kitchen. "Why the car over here? Over there better, where everybody see!"

Emilio laughed. He stopped to squeeze his mother's arm.

"That's cheap stuff. That's the bohunk show-off. It's more dignified this way. Nobody likes the world to know every time they have to see a doctor." He pinched Giustina's cheek and went on through the house to go out the front way. In the living room he came upon Elena. He winked and was about to go by. Then he turned suddenly. "What's the matter now?"

"I wonder," Elena said.

Emilio struggled to hide his confusion by working himself into a temper. But Giustina had followed him into the room. He lowered his eyes from Elena and went out of the house. "You see!" Giustina explained after she had watched Emilio cross the street. "Is low class show off how much money you make—the good luck what you have. Is cheap people do thing like this. In the blood Emilio have the gentlaman."

Elena had nothing to say. She sat down at the desk and stared at the fine-ruled lines of the open ledger. Her mother gave up in despair and returned to her housework but spent most of the time at the dining-room window, gazing proudly across the street at her son's house. When she had occasion to pass through the living room again she found Elena gone. "Elena! Elena!" she called through the house and there was no answer. She looked at the account books and the pile of bills and receipts which had not yet been entered into their proper columns. In the hallway closet she saw Elena had taken her coat. "Such girl!" she mumbled angrily. "She need the doctor too. Everything for the bizaness she leave and go outside someplace. No use. Better she find somebody and get marry before she make the whole family poor."

When Nick recognized Elena coming up the hill he limped to greet her. He led her to the pile of junk and swept his.arm in a wide gesture. "Everything what make the place look bad we throw away. From now you see the differenza. No more like before. No more anybody can say dirty, stinky place, Wop-Roost."

"You see," Beppo said. "When we finish the clean, even from the ground you can eat."

Elena smiled. "Maybe you papa lend one truck so we take this stuff to the dump someplace?" Tony asked. "Be nice if he do that for up here. Only take lilla while. We all help load up."

"I'll see if there's a truck free tomorrow and send it up with one of the men," Elena answered. She turned to Nick again. "Where is Marco?"

"Marco?" Nick looked around, puzzled. "Is long time I no see him. Was work right here with everybody." He cupped his hands to his lips. "Ho, Marco!" and waited for the echo to die away. "Where he can go?" Then he said slyly, "Salamangonia, I betch is some new ideas he work now. That fellow got the brain never stop to think. Just like the machine. Make everybody tired around here." He laughed. "Come on, we go up the house. I betch we find him there."

Elena followed Nick to Giuseppe's shack and waited. Nick came out almost immediately, slicing the tip of his chin with the back of his hand. "Nobody home. Just Angelina. She no feel good today and she sleep." He went over to the chicken coop, unlatched the door and peered inside. He closed the door again. "But was here! Jeasuma Christ, we work together clean up the junk. Is no like the smoke he can go away in the air!" He called again. He put his fingers in his mouth and whistled, a shrill blast.

"Never mind," Elena said. "It wasn't really anything. Nothing important." But her voice was listless, without energy or life.

Nick tried to make excuses. He made sure none of the other Italians was near and then said in an excited whisper, "You wait! He be here. I sure he be here right away. He got the pencil-pitch for the farm. All afternoon yesterday we work. You see everything nice, just what we gonna do. You see if is no good propozish for you family. Tch! I wonder where he can go?"

"I only wanted to talk to him," Elena repeated as if excusing herself. Nick followed her to the road, still speaking in his hoarse, confidential whisper which could be heard a hundred feet away. "And we have tell nobody. Nobody. Just me and Marco we know. We wait for you to say everything okay, and then we tell. Pretty soon you know, huh? Because is many things to talk. Lilla things, you know. But must be settle foist. Bizaness is bizaness. Poogh! I no have to tell you for the bizaness."

"I can't say anything yet for sure," Elena replied. "You'll have to wait awhile longer. Just a few days. Good-by." She left Nick in the middle of the road with a pained expression on his face. Passing the others, she waved half-heartedly and went on down to the village.

For a while Nick watched her. He moved over to the edge of the road and peered through the trees on the hillside to where the road twisted and came back again to meet the village, following her with his eyes until she was gone. Then, as if suddenly realizing Elena had come and was gone again, he began to dash about like an animated beer keg, bellowing for Marco and whistling. He ran here and there. He looked in the chicken coop again and got down on his hands and knees to have a glance under the foundation of the house. He looked everywhere and then began all over again, forgetting about his bad knee, until, out of exhaustion, he had to sit down. As his friends gathered around he said in a heavy voice, "The ground open up and swallow him. Is the only thing I can figure. Or maybe—maybe——" He couldn't bring himself to say the rest.

16

IN THE AFTERNOON the sky turned to deep gray. Billowy clouds came up out of the west and went hurtling across the heavens like smoke before the wind. Everyone prepared for a bad snowstorm. In the waiting room of his house Emilio switched on the reading lamp and turned his attention once more to the medical book which lay open on the table before him. At his left an ash tray filled with the stubs of cigarettes he had smoked and crushed during the past few hours. Now and then he put the medical book down and got up to have a look at the weather.

From the rear of the house there came to him the firm, low-heeled footsteps of the nurse as she moved about, and her voice, soft yet irritating because of its positiveness and its masculine timbre. Presently her stumpy figure appeared in the doorway of the consultation room. She looked at a little gold watch pinned to the breast of her uniform and said, "It's almost three o'clock, Doctor. The patient seems to feel fine. Do you think it's all right for her to go now?"

"Yes, I suppose so," Emilio said, getting up and checking the time with his own watch. "She's rested long enough. I'll run over and get the car. You drive? It might be a good idea, at least back to town. Give her a chance to pull herself together."

The nurse nodded and went out again. Emilio put on his hat and went running across the street. When he came back he thrashed his arms and smiled at the slim, somewhat frightened-faced girl sitting in the chair he had just vacated. The girl had opened her purse for her compact. She was pale and her hand trembled a little as she held the mirror before her eyes. "It's kicking up cold again," Emilio said. "Looks like we're in for a bad stretch of weather. Well, how do you feel?"

"All right, except a little weak," the girl said. Her voice was weak, too, and uncertain, as if she didn't know herself just how she felt or was expected to feel.

Emilio offered her a cigarette. She took it and hungrily breathed the smoke into her lungs. Then Emilio locked his hands behind his back in a true professional pose. "It's the shock more than anything. Any operation entails certain hazards. The heart is the thing we have to watch. But you're fit as a fiddle. Tomorrow you won't even know what happened." He laughed. "I've taken every precaution.

Done my very best. Why, I've known of girls who go through this sort of thing as routine and go to work the same day. Of course that's something quite different. But I can assure you there is nothing to worry about in your case. Everything has been done. I'm satisfied."

"And there's no need for me to come back here again?"

"None at all. In any case, you can always call me. But I'll see you around. Hazel Lambertson tells me you're a friend of hers. I was with her the other night at the club when she spoke to you, though I guess you were too distraught to notice. We were going to have a drink with Clara Smedly and Joe Simons. A swell couple. Sorry you couldn't come along. We had an amusing evening."

"But—but," the girl faltered, "I didn't know that. Doctor Stone didn't tell me——"

"Know what? Oh, you mean about Hazel Lambertson and myself?" Emilio laughed again. "When I saw Doctor Stone yesterday he was so concerned over you there wasn't room for him to think about anything else. Your family is certainly fortunate to have a physician like Stone. There's a man I admire. Someday I hope—— Anyway, he's asked me to join the club. I'll be proud to belong to an organization with a membership of men like Doctor Stone. Here, let me help you up."

He hurried to take her arm as the nurse appeared, dressed in her mannish coat and carrying her black leather satchel. The girl allowed Emilio to help her to her feet. Then, in a motion to smother her cigarette in the ash tray, she gently pulled away. She let the nurse go on ahead to the car. Then she said, "I'll arrange everything with Doctor Stone. You can see him. I'll leave your check there."

"That's all right. I'm not worried about that. Take care of yourself. I'd advise you to go to bed early tonight. And better let the nurse drive back to town. Good-by. We'll be running into each other again soon, I hope." He was about to hold out his hand, but the girl had already moved to open the door. Emilio waited until the car started moving, half expecting her to turn and look back, but she seemed busy explaining something about the car to the nurse. Emilio shrugged his shoulders and closed the door. He stretched his arms high over his head in a yawn which ended in a low, rollicking laugh. "Five hundred bucks! Boy, oh boy!"

He paraded into the consultation room, to the telephone, pausing to hum a tune and beat drums on top of the desk with his fists. He picked up the telephone and called Dr Stone at his residence. He tried the hospital and after a long wait managed to get him. "Hello," he said cheerfully, "this is Gardella. Everything fine. The patient went home a few minutes ago. Yes. No complications. See you sometime tomorrow. What? In the morning probably. I have a date later in the day. So long."

He put the receiver down and marched through the house again, thoroughly satisfied with himself. He poured a straight drink of whisky and sipped it slowly. When he had finished he ran his tongue around the inside of the glass and licked his lips. Then he went back to the desk to make another call. This time his approach was entirely different. First he seated himself comfortably with his feet up on the desk. He placed the dialing apparatus in his lap and delicately turned the numbers one after the other, a slight pause between each flip of the finger. There was a grin on his face as he waited for the ring at the other end of the wire.

A knock echoed through the house from the front door. He put the receiver down. "Who is it?" he called, getting up. "Nuts," as he went to the door and yanked it open, expecting to see his mother there or Elena or somebody equally unimportant. But when he saw the huge figure in a black soiled overcoat barring the doorway he drew back, startled. "What do you want?"

"I want to speak with you," Marco answered quietly. His cap was pulled down over his ears and his hands were in his pockets. His face had a bluish-red color and there was a numb, glassy texture to his skin, indicating he had been walking around in the cold a long time. Emilio kept his eyes on the bulge of Marco's pockets. After some hesitation he stepped aside. "Okay," he said. "Say what you got to say and get it over with quick. I'm busy."

He edged back into the waiting room. When he saw Marco pull out his hands and rub them together his confidence returned, the arrogance. "Come on! This is no hangout! No place for bums here, if that's what you're looking for. What do you want?"

Marco continued to rub his hands. He cupped his hands over his ears, all the while looking at Emilio. On his face the undecided expression, finding it difficult to gather the words he wanted. "For me to speak is hard," he began. "It is not my place to come here and tell you what you should do, or what you should not do. I do not believe in that when it has to do with a man and a woman. But what I am trying to do is to save you trouble and to save the suffering of a girl who is very much in love with you. It is not me and you now. Between us everything is the same as before. It is the girl Angelina. What happened, I do not know. But she is feeling very bad."

"Go on," Emilio said. "Keep it up. This is good."

"So bad," Marco went on, "that surely it will not be long before her father and her uncle know everything."

"Know what? What's there to know? Don't make me laugh!"

"Just yesterday Nick told me if anything goes wrong between you and Angelina he would take care of it himself. Do you know what that means? It means you will marry Angelina. You can laugh. But when you have lived like me with people like Nick you know that it is not to laugh. It is the family. It is the question of honor which maybe you do not understand. The law means nothing. It does not scare men like Nick. If it is necessary he will kill you. And he will go to the electric chair happy because the wrong has been made right and the family can hold up the head again."

"Well I'll be a sonofabitch!" Emilio gasped. "You have the nerve to come down here and pull——"

"Shut up!" Marco said. For an instant he flared. Then he quieted again. He sat down in a chair and crumpled his cap in his fist. "Let me talk while I am calm. Do not get me into a fight with you on this question where I have no business to mix up."

"If it's none of your business what the hell are you giving your two cents for?"

"Because," Marco said, "because I do not believe in the old system of forcing the marriage. Because I think I know what kind of a man you are and I would like to save this girl from something which might spoil her whole life."

Emilio applauded. "Jesus God! This is wonderful! Marvelous! Better than a circus!"

Marco ignored him. He unfolded his cap and stared at the lining, dark with the grime of sweat and dust. "What you have done is nothing new or original. It is just the attitude of the smart fellow that makes it something different. Angelina is in love with you. She is just a little girl. If you are gentle, if you let her go easy, little by little make her understand you are not in love with her, she will find somebody else. I am sure of that. You will save yourself all the trouble and you will make it much more easy for her. But this way?" He raised his hand. "It will not work. It will end bad for you."

Emilio listened with his hands on his hips. There was the embarrassed smirk and the crimson of anger reaching to the tips of his ears. He took a few steps across the room, whirled and came back again. He stretched his arm and pointed his finger. His lips were quivering. "I've listened to you. Now you listen to me you—you goddamn whatever you are. I don't know why they kicked you out of Italy but I know it's sonsabitches like you that make it necessary to have guys like Mussolini. You telling me what to do? You with the smell of the freight cars and all the filthy flop joints in the country, coming here and pulling the moral stuff! Where the hell do you come off? Bastards like you on the road, living off everybody else—the dregs of society. What do you take me for? Do I look like one of those goddamn fools up on the hill? Oh no! Not me. You're talking to an intelligent man now. Scare me? Scare nothing. I was born in this country. Raised here. I do what I want and as I want. And you or any other half-assed foreigner isn't going to tell me. Get the hell out of here!"

Marco didn't move. He smiled and twisted the peak of his cap. "Now I am interested for myself. It is not every day I have the chance to talk with a real American or to understand somebody like you. Tell me some more. Tell me if it is American to spit on the fellow who is not so fortunate as you. Tell me if it is American to hate everything from the people you represent because it might help you to do what you want to do. Tell me if it is American to look down on the Italian when it is just lucky that you were born here and not on the other side, and live in this house instead of up on the hill. I would like to know."

"I'll tell you," Emilio cried. "I'll tell you if you don't get out of my house, I'll throw you out! Lucky, my ass! Everything I got I worked for. I gave something for it. I owe nobody nothing, while you, you sonofabitch, coming over here without any idea of becoming Americanized, just sponging along, busting into people's houses, eating their food, poking your nose into everything——" Now Emilio's fists were clenched. "You think I'm not wise to your game. Playing the saint, and in the meantime you fill your gut, screw around behind everybody's back, and then come down here and try to make me the fall guy as if I was born yesterday and——"

"Just one minute!" Marco shouted, springing from the chair. "The last part! What do you mean by that?"

"You know damn well what I mean. Angela, I mean. You haven't fooled around with her yourself, I suppose? Ah, for Christ sake, don't——"

Marco's fist swung around. The bony mass caught Emilio square on the mouth. His head bobbed back. He gasped and fell on his knees, clutching at his face. Marco stood over him. "You, you sonofabitch, you! One more word like that and I kill you for fair!" His voice was hoarse, rasping, his entire body quivered. He grabbed up his cap and made for the door, slamming it after him.

As he turned away from the house Elena came running from across the street, hatless, her coat thrown about her shoulders. She caught his arm. "What are you doing here? What did you want with my brother?"

Marco pulled away. "I want nothing from your brother! I want nothing from the family of a brother like that!" He stopped long enough to say this and walked on again, his head in the air, his jaw set and his eyes straight before him.

Elena stared after Marco, helpless, confused. She turned to look across the street, at her mother leaning out of the window and yelling, "What he want, that bum here? What bizaness he have with Emilio?" Then she rushed up the steps to the porch and into the house. She found Emilio leaning against the mantel of the fireplace with a handkerchief pressed to his lips. She drew his hand away and saw the red, blotched swelling and the blood in his teeth. "What happened? Speak, for heaven sake!" A flood of words came into his throat and caught there. He remained with the handkerchief against his lips and the blur in front of his eyes.

Angela had told everything. Marco found Giuseppe slumped against the wall, his hands helpless at his sides, while Nick cursed and shouted and rushed back and forth across the room. "Dirty skunk! He pay, Emilio! You make him pay! You no listen before. You no listen nobody. And now when comes the result you stand like the lilla baby with the face white. Watch you gonna do? Speak! Watch you gonna do?"

Giuseppe looked as if his legs were about to cave in. Marco sat down onto the cot. He ran his hand through his hair. "What can anybody do?" he said. Nick stopped in the middle of the floor. "And you? Where you run away this morning? Where you run away this afternoon? You down there with that family and now you say, what we gonna do? I show you what we gonna do." He rushed to grab up Giuseppe's shotgun, but Marco sprang from the cot and wrested it from him. He pushed Nick aside angrily. "With the gun you will make him marry Angelina! With the gun you will make the happiness for this girl! You are crazy!"

For the moment Nick was taken off guard. Giuseppe looked from one to the other, trying to understand. Then Nick's jaws gaped apart and he nodded his head slowly. "So, is for this the farm and the nice talk what they gonna do down there for the people up here? Now I begin to onderstand. Now I see everything."

Giuseppe looked up, questioning. Nick turned to him. "This you did not know. The farm that they want to give to Marco and me. For the people up here. Is to keep the mouth close. Is to turn the eyes someplace else. Is why he no want to see any trooble. Is why he no care what happen Angelina. Is because something like this spoil everything for him." Facing Marco again, his features became a mask of loathing.

"Is true, this?" Giuseppe asked.

Marco went over to Giuseppe. "This is what is true: I have spoken with Doctor Emilio just now. For the first time I know him just like he is. And I tell you this. If you make him marry Angelina you will do something bad.

This man is no good and he will die no good. And if he lives or he dies, nobody will care. And you will force him to marry your daughter? For me, I would rather anything happens but that you do not do this thing."

"And is you will marry Angelina?" Nick shouted. "And is you will marry the girl after somebody else? Like hell you do that! Like hell anybody want the wife has fool around before!"

"And why not?" Marco said. "If I am in love I do not care what is in the past. It is just the beginning for Angelina. She is young. In the man she made the mistake. Everybody can make a mistake. Who will remember? And what will the man care who really loves her, if he knows? Love is more than that. And if it is not more than that it is not worth to be called love. But do this for me. Bring Angelina out here. Ask her if she wants to marry a man who does not love her. Ask her if she wants a man who has been making a joke of her and her people. You ask her that first."

Now Nick planted himself between Marco and Giuseppe. "We ask nobody nothing. We know what it is to do. It is Doctor Emilio do the right thing or he pay with the blood. Giuseppe!" he cried. "Dio, Giuseppe! Wake up! Is now to see if you are the man! Is now to see if somebody bring shame into you house and what you do. Tell this bum get out! Tell this man who say he is you friend and then you find it is just for his pocket he look. Angelina? What he care for Angelina? It is just Elena Gardella he have the eyes and what he can get from down there and what he can do to make it better for him."

Still Giuseppe didn't answer. Marco went over to a chair in a corner of the room, gathered his few belongings and stuffed them into the pocket of his overcoat. "I will go," he said. "I will go." He spoke directly to Giuseppe, ignoring Nick, who stood to one side, bloated and angry. "But you will remember. You will remember what I say today. Nick is wrong. It is a different country here and a different time. It is not the blood and the force that will fix anything. And if you listen to Nick it is like you take Angelina and nail her to the cross." His voice fell a little. "You have been very good to me here. I am sorry the end is to be like now. But it is the only way I can think. Even the good things you have done for me cannot make me feel different. Most of all I am sorry for Angelina because I only see that you will hurt her life in a way that maybe can never be fixed again." He hesitated at the door, watching Giuseppe, who turned away. "Go on!" Nick said. "Hurry up! Maybe in the house down there you find better eat and better sleep. Maybe you marry the girl, and when the papa die he leave you all the money. Go ahead, the rich people. Leave the poor Italiano on the hill his trooble. You no belong here. Via!"

17

THE OMINOUS SMUDGE of night coming on. No sun sinking in the west and no gilded reflections. Only a deepening gradation of somber tones and the whistling wind so that from the hill the village below appeared like a forlorn cluster of houses on a barren, toneless plain. Marco stepped away from Giuseppe's house and onto the road, turning up the collar of his coat and pulling the peak of his cap down low over his forehead. Giuseppe's little black-and-tan hound came running and he paused to pick the dog up in his arms, rubbing its soft, flappy ears. He laughed. "Good-by, you, funny face." He set the dog down and slapped its flank, then started slowly along the road to the village. As he passed each tar-paper-covered shack, sitting so rigid and cold against the oncoming night, he paused. Tony's shack and little shrimp Tony inside with

the monkey face and the five-cent pipe! Luca's shack and
Luca with his spaghetti belly and his pants always falling
down! He turned to look back. Nick, and Giuseppe, far
away now, out of sight of the window. Then, further along,
he saw Vincenzo just sitting down to dinner with his wife
and son. Vincenzo, skinny like a string bean and with the
liver like a chicken! Even Vincenzo!

Marco dug his hands deep into his pockets and bit the
corner of his lip. He went on. Now at his back the shacks
and ahead the village. The wind lashed at his face and he
had to turn aside. Over to the left, in the lot, he could see
the empty barn, leaning at an angle and the doors rocking.
He shivered, looked up at the sky, at the deepening black-
ness there and his jaw set tight. An impulse hurried him
along, closer to the village. He opened his coat and
searched through the pockets of his trousers, counting a
dime, several pennies and a key. He held the key in his
hand for some time, staring at it, his gaze following along
the street to Emilio's house and the warm, illuminated
windows of the Gardella dwelling. He started forward, the
wind coming at him and with it a few scattered flakes of
snow. In front of the house he stood undecided for a moment. Then he clenched the key in his fist and walked
back along the sidewalk.

He went into the grocery store and bought a loaf of
bread. He put the bread under his arm and headed toward
Wop-Roost again, this time avoiding the road, cutting up
the side of the hill through the shadowy trees and coming

out again past Giuseppe's house. As he moved along, down
the other side of Wop-Roost, Giuseppe's dog shot in front
of him again. "Come on," he called. "Come on, puppy. For
tonight you will keep me company. Tomorrow I will worry
what to do." He turned from the road to cross the field
where the bleak outline of Gardella's abandoned farmhouse
rose in the distance.

After closeting himself in the house for more than an
hour, nursing his swollen lip, Emilio went over to the drugstore. He found the druggist's wife behind the counter,
an emaciated little woman with red-tinted hair and a
powdery, chalklike complexion. "Where's George?" he
asked.

"He's been gone most of the afternoon. Went to Terry-
ville," the woman answered. "He ought to be back pretty
soon now, if he don't get drunk and fall asleep on the road
someplace. What—what happened to your face?"

"Nothing," Emilio said. "I bunked myself, that's all."
He leaned across the soda fountain and studied his face in
the mirror, stretching his lip with the tip of his tongue.
"I'm going to stay in town for the night. Tell him to give
me a ring at the Madden Hotel. I want to talk to him."

"I'll tell him," the druggist's wife said. She looked at
Emilio's lip again and smiled. Emilio turned away and
walked out of the store. In front of his father's house he
drew a deep breath, marched quickly up the steps and
entered without bothering to take off his hat or his hands

out of his pockets. Giustina rushed up to him. Her eyes showed fear and her cheeks were stained from crying. She shook his arm. "Why you lock youself in the house? Why you chase Elena away? What happen inside there with that fellow? Santo Dio, you face all swoll up!" She verged on tears again. Elena came into the room and then Federico. Elena moved close, anxious, excited to hear everything, but Federico remained apart, standing in a corner, watching.

Emilio pulled away from his mother. "Pack my suitcase with my tuxedo, my stiff shirt and some clean laundry. I'm going to stay in town tonight, tomorrow night too."

"Why?" Giustina cried. "Why you gotta go away?"

Emilio lowered his head like a charging bull. "I'll tell you why. I'm getting out of here now to keep myself from going up there and killing that dirty bastard hobo. That's why I'm going." He came to life and strode across the living room, flinging his arms around. "Imagine that guinea punk laying his hands on me? I'll kill him! I'll take the gun and go up there and blow his goddamn brains out!"

"You go the electric chair!" Giustina screamed, pressing his hand to her breast. "Call the police. They put him in the prison! But no you kill him youself."

"Stop all the theatricals," Elena said. "Why did he hit you? There must have been some reason!"

"Sure there's a reason. There's the reason that he's been playing around with Angela and now he comes down here to try and switch the blame onto me. I should be nice to her, he says. I should do this and I should do that. And I listened to him! Instead of busting his head open with the floor lamp, I gave him a chance to take a sock at me. Jesus Christ Almighty!"

"I don't believe it."

Now Emilio whirled on his sister. "You don't believe what? What did you say?"

"I said I don't believe Marco ever had anything to do with Angela, that's what I said."

"Why, you little snot nose, you're just as bad as he is. I'll——" He raised the flat of his hand to slap her.

"Put the hands down!" Federico shouted. He barged forward, two hundred pounds of beef across the room at Emilio, his cheeks the color of fire and shaking his pudgy fists. "You touch anybody here, I break you in half." Giustina came to interfere and with a swipe of his arm he brushed her aside. "Now you talk! Then after I talk myself. What they want from you up on the hill?"

Emilio grew sullen. He refused to answer. He backed away, glowering at his father and cursing under his breath. "I tell you what they want. They want you marry Angelina," Federico said. "That what the big fellow come down to talk." He turned from Emilio to his wife, watching the horror come into her face.

"I'll marry her," Emilio said. "Like hell I'll marry her. What have they got on me? What can they prove? You think I'm worried? Let the whole goddamn Wop-Roost come down and try and make me do a anything I don't want to do." Now as he raised his voice he grew bolder, more confident. "This is a free country here. They got to prove I had something to do with the damn girl. And they got to prove it was me and not somebody else. That vendetta stuff don't work here. Just let them so much as touch me——"

Giustina took up the cry. "Dirty lilla bum! Is trick. Is lie to catch Emilio. I see how she go after him. I see myself from the window how she wait outside the house and walk up and down and follow him every place. The proof! Where the proof he want anything to do with her? Is here. Is me the proof that she chase him like a dog with the tongue hang out. Is me the proof she want doctor for hoosband and she make any kind trick for to get him." She took her place alongside Emilio, her little shriveled figure a seething, furious defense.

"So, is the proof you want," Federico said. He nodded his head. The interval of silence became tense. Elena moved nearer. Emilio and Giustina stood motionless. A subtle change came over Emilio as he watched his father. "Is the proof," slowly, "that last night you have Angelina in you house. You have her in you bed. And I am the proof because I hear everything from under the window."

Back at the house Emilio threw his suitcase on the bed and crammed into it the articles of dress he would need for a few days. "They'll get me! Like hell they'll get me! My whole life! My whole goddamn future on that little bitch.

They can all rot, up there and down here!" He slammed
the suitcase shut and carried it into the waiting room.
Here he set the suitcase down again, nervously pounding
his fist into his palm. He fell into a chair, lit a cigarette
and threw the match on the floor. He took deep, quick
puffs, smoking the cigarette down to his fingers and then
crushing the butt under his heel. He remained for a long
time, his hands gripping the arms of the chair, his head
thrown back and his breath coming in heavy spasms.

When he got up finally, he put out all the lights and
locked the door. Now the snow had really begun, forming
whirling, dancing eddies against the curbstone outside.
First he peered along the sidewalk through the filmy haze,
dropped the suitcase on the porch and hurried across the
street to the drugstore. He entered just as the druggist's wife
was going out and the druggist was putting on his white
coat to get behind the counter. "Hello, Emile," the druggist said. "I was just going to call up your old man." Then
the snow attracted his attention and he grinned. "Made it
just in time. Drove like hell all the way back from Terry-
ville. Took the back road. You know me how I like to put
on chains? Say, who smacked you in the puss?"

Emilio waited until the druggist's wife had closed the
door. "Never mind the face. Never mind about you and
your chains. I heard that about fifty times already this
winter. I'm in a mess, George. Angela. She spilled the
beans. It's all over the hill and my old man knows I had
her in the house last night. They're trying to rope me into

a shotgun wedding. They think they can force me to marry her."

"Holy Moses!" the druggist gasped. Then he added, "I told you! I told you! You had to go and stick your neck out. You're never satisfied. You gotta push a thing and push it until it snaps back in your face. Now what you gonna do? And you never stopped to figure she ain't eighteen yet. Oh lord!"

"Go ahead," Emilio said. "Fancy it up. Make it better. It isn't bad enough now. But you think I'm going to fall for this gag? You're crazy like all the rest of them. And it's that hobo again in back of it all. I'll murder him and every other wop in the country before they can make me go through with this. Now listen. It all isn't as bad as it sounds. I know the dago temperament. Fireworks and excitement and then everything peters out. I'll just shove off for a couple of days until things quiet down—until my old man cools off. Anyway, I got a date tomorrow night, so what the hell's the difference? But here's what I want you to do. I'll get a room over at the Madden Hotel and you keep your eyes open. Let me know if anything happens. Watch my house. I'd like to know if those bastards 'll really try anything."

"That's easy. Just stay here and find out for yourself."

"You go to hell. If I'm here it 'll only make things worse. They'll realize they can't marry a girl off to a guy if he doesn't want her. They got brains enough to see that. But you phone if you hear anything. Okay?"

The druggist agreed in a manner which showed he didn't like the idea very much. Emilio squeezed his arm. "Thanks. You're a pal." Then to change the subject he said, "What did you start to say about getting in touch with my father? Christ, don't talk to him now. He's fit to be tied."

"It's nothing," the druggist said. "Only when I was coming along up the back road I saw a light in that old farmhouse you people own over the hill. First I thought the place was on fire and I stopped. Then I could see it was the fireplace going. Must be a couple of tramps busted in."

"Tramps!" Emilio said. "More tramps! The goddamn place is overrun with hobos. Where they all come from? I'll be a sonofabitch, I don't know what the country's coming to. Here." He tossed a nickel down on the counter. "Don't bother the old man. Call up the state police and have them investigate. That's their job. That's all we need now, for them to burn the house down. Damnit-the-hell." He moved toward the door. "I better scram now. Don't forget. Let me know anything right away." He grabbed the doorknob and pulled the door open, but suddenly his body stiffened. He turned around again, all the blood rushing from his face, his eyes wide in their sockets.

The druggist got scared. "What's come over you? Why you looking at me like that?"

"Marco!" Emilio said in a breath. "It couldn't be him there in the farmhouse, could it?"

"How do I know? You don't get a million hobos around

in this section every day. It could and it couldn't. Maybe he got in a scrap up there and they kicked him out? What are you gonna do?"

"It couldn't be," Emilio repeated. "It just couldn't be." However, his face was shining like a man riding a beautiful dream. He reached out his hand. "Quick. Give me that nickel. Hurry up." The druggist handed him the coin and he rushed to the back of the store to the phone booth. The druggist saw him dial the operator and ask for the state police. Then Emilio closed the door.

When Emilio came out of the booth he was in a cold sweat. He removed his hat. He sat down at the soda fountain and passed his hand across his forehead and reached over the fountain to fill a glass with seltzer. He looked at his wrist watch. "From the station house on the parkway! Those troopers ought to be here in a couple of minutes." He drank the seltzer and got up again. "If it is him. If it is I'll have the dirty skunk right where I want him. He'll hit me! He'll raise his hands to me! He'll interfere with people better than himself! He'll stew in jail and every word he ever spoke will come up from his guts and make him vomit." He turned to the druggist, the trembling, uncontrollable anger again. "Where are those guys? When you want them they never come. They sit on their cans all day long, riding around like Northwest Mounted in the movies. The bastards are quick enough to give you a ticket, but call them for something, just call them for something, and then see how quick they are."

"Give them time," the druggist said. "It's a rotten night outside. The snow is beginning to pile up. So he took a smack at you?"

"What's the snow got to do with it? When somebody calls me I go out. The snow doesn't stop me. The time of the night. It's my job. I understood that before I started. You do your job or you don't do it. You give something to this world or you're just a goddamn parasite crawling across the face of the earth. That's the way I see it."

"All right. All right. You don't have to get sore. I didn't say anything."

A woman came in and walked over to the prescription counter, nodding to the druggist and then to Emilio. She wanted some kind of salve for burns. As the druggist looked over his stock supplies she confided to Emilio. "Willie, he spilled the boiling kettle over himself and scalded his chest something awful."

"Give her some tannic acid," Emilio said to the druggist; "that's the best thing. Here, you take a little bit like this and mix it in a cup of warm water. Then with absorbent cotton you apply it to the burns. You keep doing that and you'll see that everything'll be fine. That's all right. Don't mention it."

The woman went out, bowing and smiling her gratitude. The druggist returned to the soda fountain and Emilio started once more his exasperating parade across the floor, all the while watching the clock. "Stop it!" the druggist said. "You give me the jitters. They'll be here any minute now."

"They'll be here! They'll be here! In the meantime I could have gone up there myself and yanked that punk out in the snow to freeze. Oh, what the hell!"

A car pulled up in front of the drugstore. They could see it through the driving snow, white, with the brown side curtains all around and the black lettering on the door, "State Police," superimposed upon the official seal. There were two troopers in the car. One of them got out and came inside, tall, handsome in his beaver hat with the crystal particles of snow clinging to it, his sheepskin coat and black leather mittens. He saluted Emilio. "Did you make the call about somebody breaking into a house?"

"Yes," Emilio said. "My name is Gardella. Doctor Emile Gardella. You've probably seen my shingle across the street. My friend here tells me he saw a light tonight in a farmhouse my family owns. I'd like you to investigate."

"What's it, a vacant farmhouse?"

Emilio nodded. The trooper turned from him to glance out through the glass door. But he didn't say anything. "Okay. We'll investigate."

"You keep on straight," Emilio said. "Up over the hill and down again. When you hit the valley you'll come to a little bridge. There's a lane on the right, just about fifty yards further on, and the house sets back a ways. Let me know what you find."

The trooper saluted again and went out. Emilio watched him through the door as he swept his hand over the windshield and got into the car, beside the driver. Then the vehicle moved off and there were only the marks of its wheels in the settling whiteness, the snow driving against the glass door, coming faster and faster all the time, and the wind increasing. Emilio was silent now. Behind the counter the druggist leaned on his elbows. "He'll get away, whoever it is. He'll hear the car coming and beat it out through the window. Maybe they'll take a shot at him. I heard of hobos getting killed like that more than once."

"So they'll shoot him. What the hell business has he got trespassing on private property and breaking into a house? What are laws made for if anyone can come along and break them? What about the rights of property and ownership? A few lessons here and there and you'd see there wouldn't be so goddamn much of the monkey business we have in this country these days." He stood near the door, pressing his fist against the glass and rocking on his heels. He went over to the shelves of the circulating library, picked out a book, opened the cover and put it back again. Finally in exasperation he said, "For Christ sake, say something. Do you have to stand there as if you were a dummy?"

"What you want me to say? That you got yourself in a jam and I don't know how the hell you're going to get out of it? Your old man! He's a big fat, good-natured guy. But once I seen him get mad and go for one of his men with a pick. He meant business too. If he got the idea you should marry Angela, you'll find yourself out on your tail. Giuseppe don't mean nothing, but that Nick is a hotheaded bastard too. You worked it perfect all right. And with everything all set for you in town! You're one prize jackass, if I ever saw one."

"Go ahead, rub it in! Rub it in!" Emilio turned up his collar and went outside, standing in the entrance to the drugstore, his back to the wind, the snow slanting over his shoulder, and trying to see along the road leading up the hill and over Wop-Roost. He remained outside for some time, then stamped his feet and slapped the snow from his coat and returned to get warm. He removed his gloves and blew into his fists. "What takes them so long?" he said. "It doesn't take that long to go over the hill and back again." In a few minutes he put on his gloves and went back outside again. This time he walked through the snow and up the street a little distance. He came running back. "Here they come now! I can see the headlights shooting over the hill!"

He was breathless, excited. He didn't know what to do. When the car pulled up he walked nervously to the back of the store before going outside. As the driver stretched across the seat to open the door of the car Emilio saw the trooper sitting in back and Marco at his side. Their eyes met. For an instant he felt the scornful, penetrating look. Then Emilio and the driver went back into the drugstore, the policeman reaching into his pocket for a pad and pencil. "He had a dog with him," the trooper said, "and he

made us stop up on the top of the hill to drop the mutt.
You know him?"'

"I'll say. He's been hanging around here about a week,
living off everybody. The first night he came into the store
here and tried to steal from the counter. That right,
George?"

The druggist nodded. After the trooper had asked several questions about the farm and its owner Emilio said,
"What can he get on a thing like this?"

The trooper put the edge of the pad to his lips. "For
vagrancy, about ten days. But if he goes up for house-
breaking, that's a felony. That could mean a ride of a
couple of years. But there was nothing disturbed, though.
He just had a fire going to keep warm. And there was no
sign of having broken in."

"The hell he didn't break in. The door was locked. I
know. I locked it myself the last time I was up there. He
must have picked the lock or forced a window. It's the
only way he could have gotten in."

"All right," the trooper said. "It's up to you."

"Sure it's up to me. These guys going around so nothing
is safe any more! Suppose the place got on fire and burned
down, where would we be?"

The trooper nodded. He didn't say anything further,
simply put away his pad and pencil, raised his hand in a
brisk salute and went out. Emilio waited inside the door
until the car was in motion again. Then he rushed out to
watch it disappear, its headlights flaring against the curtain

of driving snow. The druggist joined him and Emilio said, "There! That takes care of him. Now let's see if all the rest of them together up there can put anything over on me." He laughed and slapped the druggist on the shoulder. "So long, George! Take it easy. I'll see you in a couple of days."

The druggist waited until Emilio had crossed the street and turned back to the warmth of his store.

18

FEDERICO'S ANGER had spent itself. He lay on the couch with his heels dug into the pillows, his collar unbuttoned and his arms under his head. A mountain of man lying there on the living-room sofa, awake, grim, his very manner defiance to the world of his own household. He could spit on the floor. If he wanted he could tear the house down to its foundation. He could do anything out of his anger. But now he lay calm, resting—waiting.

When he got up from the sofa he staggered a bit. He hitched his belt a few notches, buttoned the collar of his shirt and walked into the dining room. Elena was at the window watching the snowstorm, while Guistina sat huddled in the rocking chair, her arms folded across her breast, her face the color of mold. But determination was still there, fixed, immobile—chiseled out of stone. The table was set and the soup cold, a thin film of grease forming on the top of each plate. Federico went over to his daughter. He observed the snow as it swept against the windowpane and the mounting drift in a corner of the sill. "You think we get up on the hill with the car tonight?" he asked.

"I don't think so," Elena said. "I wouldn't try if I were you."

"We try just the same," Federico said. "Tonight we settle this thing. The clock go. The clock go. Every minute pass the lump inside my head come more big and more big." He sighed. "Ah, Dio!" His eyes rested on Giustina for a moment. He caught a few hairs of his mustache between his teeth and bit them. "What I have become? Me, Federico Gardella! What those people think up there for me and my family?" He rocked his head. "What anybody care what those people think! The wop. Italiano, guinea. But what am I myself? What you in the chair? You wop, guinea too. And now from my house come the worst can happen. If Emilio never be doctor, if he never have one customer any more, he do what is suppose for him to do. On my mother under the ground, I swear. . . ."

Slowly Federico went over to the table. He picked up a spoon, stirred the soup in his plate and let the spoon fall. He pointed a finger at his wife. "Is no use for you to sit there with the black face. Is no use think you can save Emilio from marry Angelina, because if you try do something, if you mix two cents, I throw you out in the street.

Onderstand? Now for you is the mouth close. Elena! You
go in the garage and start up the car."

Elena didn't move. "You'll get stuck in the snow. You'll
never be able to get back."

"Stuck my nose! Do what I tell you do. Or is now with
you I have the fight too? That's all what I need. You, too,
like everybody else."

Elena went out of the room. Federico's eyes followed her,
glaring, his anger seeking a new victim for attack. He said
to Giustina, "Tonight you be very happy. Very happy. The
work for so many years finish like this. The high-class life
you have figure out for Emilio. The American wife. The
house in the town with the rich people live next door and
say to you, 'Allo, Missa Gardella. You the mamma from
Doctor Emilio?' Ah, you make the pitch nice for youself.
From lilla baby you begin him with this ideas. And me,
salamambitch fool, I listen and keep the face close. Is
you responsible for what happen now? Is you responsabila
for everything, and is me responsabila for listen to you?
What happen Emilio now? Is fine life, the man with the
wife he hate and he have to marry just the same. The man
with the wonderfool brains hold down because the chain
on his neck. And he end maybe by kill her. And is you
responsabila for this. For Angelina too. Because was no for
you push alla time the ideas make money and become high-
class American with the bad smell for the Italiano, he fall
in love with Angelina and live happy just like anybody.
And he be better doctor too. But this animale you have

raise! And me too! Is become something for to take in the woods and shoot like a dog you no can cure from eat the chicken."

Giustina hadn't moved, nor had a single line of her expression changed. Federico's words fell upon her and she remained the same, a shadowy statue of gypsum with arms folded. Now the statue swayed, rocked back and forth as if mounted on some kind of mechanical contrivance, and that was all.

The buzzer of the front door rang. Federico stood with his hand suspended in the air. The buzzer sounded again, louder, more insistent. He lowered his hand, the flush that suffused his face slowly receding. He looked at his wife and started into the living room. There was a shuffle of footsteps behind him and he rushed back, grabbing Giustina just as she was heading upstairs. He yanked her into the living room, throwing her down on the sofa. "There! There you sit. And no move! And no talk!" He went to the door.

Giuseppe came in first followed by Nick, the both of them covered with snow and tracking it into the room. Giuseppe in his hunting coat, the flaps of his cap pulled down over his ears, wearing his felt boots with the arctics over them. Nick in his black coat with the fur collar, black hat and heavy working shoes with string tied around the legs of his trousers. When Giuseppe saw Giustina he looked at his feet and turned to go back into the hall to brush the snow away. But Nick pushed him forward into the center of the room. "Is no now the time to worry for the dirty feets." He looked up at Federico. "Maybe you know why we here?"

"I know," Federico said. "You want sit down?"

"We no want sit down." Nick nudged Giuseppe. "You gonna talk or I have to talk for you?"

In Giuseppe's face there was timidity, fright and pain mixed together in one surging emotion. "Angelina," he began. "Angelina." He couldn't go any further. The name stuck in his throat as if to choke him. "Is no Angelina," Nick blared. "Is Emilio. We come to find out what he gonna do. We come first to you, the papa. If you no can tell us, then we go to him."

Giustina bit her lip and sprang up from the sofa. "First you tell where all the money from up there that belong to us!"

"Shut up!" Federico rushed at her with his hand raised. "I no tell you again!" He turned to the two men. "What you want Emilio to do? Tell me, what you expect?"

"Expect!" Nick said. "We expect nothing. Never we have expect anything. Emilio marry Angelina. Is no expect. Is sure."

Elena came into the room shaking the glistening particles of snow from her hair. She stood in a corner listening, breathless, to the tense voices. "Angelina in love with Doctor Emilio," Giuseppe said. "She love him."

"But Emilio no love Angelina," Giustina cried triumphantly. "And for that you no can do nothing."

Federico was about to interfere again, but Nick's voice roared above his own. "And that for Emilio is too bad because he will marry Angelina just the same. The love! Now after the dirty work you talk for the fine sentimento. The love! For love I no give one goddamn. If Emilio no want broke his head he do what right for Angelina." The power of his own voice carried him across the room to Giustina. "You think I afraid? You think my name is Giuseppe? Or Vincenzo? Is only for Angelina I no take the gun right now. I give him chance. Just tomorrow. If tomorrow he no say what he gonna do—if tomorrow——"

"What is to do, Emilio will do," Federico said. "That I proomise myself." He put his hand on Giuseppe's shoulder. "I am sorry, Giuseppe. Was no me want the thing happen this way. For the father I proomise Emilio marry you girl or he no come in this house no more."

Now Elena came forward, her face puzzled, bewilderment there on her brow. "Angela? What does Angela think of all this? Do you mean—is it possible she would want to marry Emilio under circumstances like this? No matter what's happened? I can't imagine. I can't see it. It would be living in hell. It would be—I don't know. I don't know what to say. . . ."

Nick laughed. "Talk. Talk. Make believe you no can onderstand. Everything you have fix nice with Marco. The farm, the whole bizaness to take the eyes from what you brother do with Angelina. Ha, ha, ha." Then his jaws snapped together. "But Marco now we have throw out. And you, you can talk and talk and talk and make everybody laugh."

"The farm?" Federico repeated. "Marco?" Even Giustina showed astonishment. Elena held up her hand to quiet her father. She stared at Nick, unbelieving. "What did you say? What happened to Marco?"

"What happen!" Nick scoffed. "You know. Call Marco. Is here in the house someplace. You think I fool? You think Marco get in trooble up on the hill just for to sleep in the snow?" His voice trailed off suddenly as he saw Elena's body slump. He watched her take a few steps and fall into the chair at the desk with her hands in her lap. "Whatsamatter?" he said.

"Is no the whatsamatter here now," Federico answered. "Marco come down this afternoon and smash his poonch in Emilio face. Like that we know what happen for Angelina."

There was a dead silence. Nick tried to say something. He turned to Giuseppe. He tried to become brave and blustering again and he could only put his thumb to his lip and press the tip of it against his teeth. He looked at Giustina, saw the slender smile without it registering anything to his brain. Federico said, "Now is better you go home. Tomorrow we will talk about Angelina and Emilio. I proomise what he will do." He led Nick and Giuseppe to the door, standing with them until they had turned up their collars and gone out into the snow. He slapped away the snow that had swirled in on him through the open door. Giustina got up quickly from the sofa and ran up-

stairs, locking herself in the bedroom. He watched Elena
for a moment, quiet at the desk. Then he slipped on his
overcoat to go and put the Packard back into the garage.

At nine-thirty the next morning Emilio was in the
barbershop of the hotel getting a shave, a haircut and a
manicure. "Just a little touching up with the scissors," he
said to the barber. "Don't use the clippers. I hate those
haircuts where you look like a convict. You know what I
mean." He was feeling good. The barber fussing with his
face and head and the girl holding his hand filled him with
a sense of well-being. Outside the snow had stopped; the
sun was trying to break through the clouds again, and the
air, filled with floating silver by the dying wind, gave the
world a magical lightness which suited his mood. "How
are the roads?" he asked. "Think I'll have any trouble driving down to the city tonight?"

"The plows have been working," the barber said. He
leaned close to Emilio's ear. "This town! All the money
appropriated for snow removal and equipment and look at
that street out there! Graft. Rotten politics, that's what it is.
What we need here is a cleanup from top to bottom just
like I been telling everybody for three years now."

Emilio laughed. "What can you do? There will always
be graft and rotten politics. That's my opinion. You can't
change human nature. Fear is the only thing that keeps all
of us with our hands clean. So there'll be a change of ad-
ministration—so what? So you'll be mixed up in it some-